The Gospel and Racial Reconciliation

Establishing the 21ˢᵗ Century Baseline for "A Long Way to Go"

Rev. Chris McNairy

Urban Fusion Network

Books

No part of this book can be reproduced, stored in a retrieval system, or transmitted by any means electronically, mechanically, photocopying, or otherwise without the expressed prior permission of the author.

Unless otherwise noted, all Scripture quotations are taken from the King James Version of the Bible. Other versions used where noted are also from the Bible Gateway. www.biblegateway.com

Copyright © 2015 Christopher McNairy

All rights reserved.

Missional Urban Fusion Books

P.O. Box 2227 Lawrenceville, Georgia 30046

ISBN-13: 978-0989591232
ISBN-10: 0989591239

Dedication

Dedicated to "all" the heroes and heroines of the Faith. We stand on your shoulders. Especially Jewell McNairy Sr., my earthly father, a great servant in the ministry of reconciliation, who experienced his "Great Consummation" with the Lord April 16, 2014.

Preface

... we possess this precious treasure [the divine Light of the Gospel] in [frail, human] vessels of earth, that the grandeur *and* exceeding greatness of the power may be shown to be from God and not from ourselves.[8] We are hedged in (pressed) on every side [troubled and oppressed in every way], but not cramped *or* crushed; we suffer embarrassments *and* are perplexed *and* unable to find a way out, but not driven to despair;[9] We are pursued (persecuted and hard driven), but not deserted [to stand alone]; we are struck down to the ground, but never struck out *and* destroyed...
2 Corinthians 4:7-9 The Amplified Bible

This book is written through the lens of a Christian disciple that happens to be a black male over half a century old. "I still have hope" – Rev. Chris McNairy February 22, 2015

Table of Contents

Introduction	When will we stop saying "we have a long way to go"	Page 8
Chapter 1	Unpacking the Gospel	Page 17
Chapter 2	Forgiveness - don't try to do life without it	Page 27
Chapter 3	Understanding Racial Reconciliation	Page 39
Chapter 4	Information Reconciliation and the African Diaspora	Page 53
Chapter 5	The Necessity of a Biblical worldview	Page 62
Chapter 6	Establishing a 21st Century Reconciliation Process	Page 77

Appendix	Page 88
Bibliography	Page 102
About the Author	Page 105
Endnotes	Page 106

Introduction

When Will We Stop Saying "We have a long way to go…"

> ¹⁸There is no fear in love; but perfect love casteth out fear: because fear hath torment. He that feareth is not made perfect in love. ¹⁹ We love him, because he first loved us. ²⁰ If a man say, I love God, and hateth his brother, he is a liar: for he that loveth not his brother whom he hath seen, how can he love God whom he hath not seen? ²¹ And this commandment have we from him, that he who loveth God love his brother also. 1 John 4:18-21

In the past few years I have offered an occasional paper annually in January. Due to this important season in American life; I felt it proper to offer this resource. This resource is directed to the body of Christ and especially to the Southern Baptist Convention, the denominational family to which I belong. I would like to offer it as a part of the framework for going forward. This book is intentionally focused more on the reconciliation of blacks (the African Diaspora) and whites (the European Diaspora) in North America. The major challenge of racial reconciliation in America is still a predominantly black and white issue.

Moreover for clarity, in this work I do not see racism and prejudice as synonyms. I am fully aware some prefer to use the terms prejudice, racially insensitive, and racism as all the same. I have a strong choice to the contrary. Racial insensitivity is a politically correct term of the reverse type that makes some sinful actions seem not sinful. Comparatively, all individuals are prejudice even within our own families and as individuals. At its root, being prejudice is not harmful.

Racism, on the other hand, based in hatred is sinfully harmful at its root and contrary to the love of God. Racism is not a sin of the skin, but sin because of the skin. Racism is perfected and continues to the extent that those who practice it deny its very existence. It is not only a sin of the past, unfortunately it has a current reality even within our institutions and yes the body of Christ. Racism can be Institutional (systematic), educational, individual and religious to name some of the ways. One can carry out racist actions without having a pattern or lifestyle of racism. Just as stealing one item is thievery, one who has a pattern or lifestyle of stealing is a thief. Particularly in the body of Christ, we should not use the words prejudice and racism interchangeably. Neither should there be patterns of racist actions among us.

Thank God for the boldness of those in the body of Christ who have called for a real present day racial reconciliation conversation[i] (especially white Christians[ii])   However, there is still too much of an 'unholy hush' when it comes to a sustained conversation that would lead to real racial reconciliation. It has been suggested that whites are tired of being made to feel guilty and blacks are tired of being considered angry. In the meantime, racial and cultural power preservation and financial considerations are restraining many from addressing the elephants in the room that crowd out the racial reconciliation conversation. These symbolic elephants are fear, racial/cultural arrogance, power preservation, and financial gain. Yes, we have made some inconsistent corporate gestures within segments of the body of Christ in America regarding racial reconciliation, but when the layers of substantial racial reconciliation are peeled back "the church' in the western hemisphere does not racially reflect a biblical picture.[iii]

In recent months and as we observed the traditional Black History Month of February 2015, it has become acceptable from most seats to frame comments regarding racial reconciliation in America (generally and in the body of Christ) with the phrase – 'we have come a long way, but we have a long way to go'. While the phrase has been used anecdotally; it has not been defined so that we might have clearer success metrics as time marches on. I have heard this phrase so much that it caused me to take a historical look in modern times at how long this same phrase has been used to describe racial reconciliation in the body of Christ.

Since the Trevon Martin case in Florida, and forward to the Michael Brown situation in Missouri, and the Eric Garner case in New York the common conversation has included the question what is the current status of race relations and racial reconciliation in America? The trend of the answer became either we have come a long, long way but we have a long, long way to go or we have come a long way but we have a long way to go. I decided to do my own survey to verify the trending of this answer. So I begin to ask people, especially blacks and whites of both genders and all ages to quantify how they see race relations and reconciliation in 21st century America. While informal and limited to the situations and peoples that I encountered over a period of months in 2014; the overwhelming answer was always some variation of we have come a long way but we have a long way to go.

The next phase of my surveying was to frame a generic question about a project that I had begun some 30 years earlier and when asked about its status my reply was I have come a long way but I have a long way to go. Fast forward to 2015, and they now asked about the status of the same project from some years ago and my response is still I have come a long way but I have a long way to go. Each person shared that they would think I had done very little if anything to complete the project. If we continue the path of non-definition regarding defining 'a long way to go' on racial reconciliation in the body of Christ, we will continue in our separated, weak, sinful positions.

There should be a difference when we examine the body of Christ compared to the world outside of the body of Christ when it comes to loving all types of peoples. We in the body of Christ should be held to a higher standard, set by biblical commands. Expectations of Biblical standards in regard to racial reconciliation are not aspirational goals to be achieved **somewhere eventually down the road**. Even today, there are too many ways in which the body of Christ (individuals, local churches and denominational families) do not lead the way when it comes to demonstrating the love that should reflect the Great Commandment. Parts of this book may seem simple to those of the academic community but it is the rank and file Christians that must carry the racial reconciliation conversation in large measure in the body of Christ.

My reflections and research also led me to a speech given by Dr. Martin Luther King, Jr. a few days before he received the Nobel Peace Prize December 7, 1964. Incidentally, at the time he was the youngest person to ever receive the award. His opening words included the following;

> ... There is a desperate, poignant question on the lips of people all over our country and all over the world. I get it almost everywhere I go and almost every press conference. It is a question of whether we are making any real progress in the struggle to make racial justice a reality in the United States of America. And whenever I seek to answer that question, on the one hand, I seek to avoid an undue pessimism; on the other hand, I seek to avoid a superficial optimism. And I try to incorporate or develop what I consider a realistic position, by admitting on the one hand that we have made many significant strides over the last few years in the struggle for racial justice, but by admitting that before the problem is solved we still have numerous things to do and many challenges to meet. And it is this realistic position that I would like to use as a basis for our thinking together tonight as we think about the problem in the United States. We have come a long, long way, but we have a long, long way to go before the problem is solved.[iv]

So on a world-wide stage back in 1964 a black Baptist preacher declared "we have come a long, long way but we have a long, long way to go". Yet, today, we cannot declare that America and/or Canada is post racial. To declare post racial societies in 2015 is uninformed at best. We have to admit that we still have a racial reconciliation problem in America's church that is unfortunately still reflective of a broader reconciliation issue. Now is not the time to be quiet and hope that racial reconciliation and its related issues will work out on their own or go away. From positions as prophets and priests, we must speak to general and specific issues. Yes, there are the general principles of God's word; but is there a "Rhema word" regarding 21st century racial reconciliation? I would say most definitely. This is not the time to be quiet in our families, in our churches, in our communities, nor nationally. This is not the time to be quiet in our varied circles of influence. It is time to have the reconciliation conversation. It is time to show the world that we are one (reconciled) in Christ Jesus.

> [9] "You're blessed when you can show people how to cooperate instead of compete or fight. That's when you discover who you really are, and your place in God's family. [10] "You're blessed when your commitment to God provokes persecution. The persecution drives you even deeper into God's kingdom. [11-12] "Not only that—count yourselves blessed every time people put you down or throw you out or speak lies about you to discredit me. What it means is that the truth is too close for comfort and they are uncomfortable. You can be glad when that happens—give a cheer, even!—for though they don't like it, *I* do! And all heaven applauds. And know that you are in good company. My prophets and witnesses have always gotten into this kind of trouble. Matthew 5:9-12 The Message (MSG)[v]

Priest comfort the afflicted. Prophets afflict the comfortable. You will only know if you are having impact if you pointed to a reality at certain seasons of the journey. It is quite telling when the same quantification depictions are used over decades, in some cases as a badge of honor. Such has become the case with the phrase, "we have come a long way, but we have a long way to go." Inadequate baselines and metrics are dangerous as one group's call for delay is another group's detriment. Moreover, conditions and data are unrelentingly stubborn and when faced head on cannot be manipulated. For the body of Christ, the mantra should be "when we learn better, we do better." We have learned, so it is now time for us to do. We are entitled to our opinions (whatever they may be); but we are not entitled to our own facts. With a clear 21st century baseline regarding racial reconciliation we can begin to earnestly move forward to looking more like the people of God and leaving legacies that provide the new pictures in present and future institutes and museums. Again I reference Martin Luther King, Jr. from the closing section of a March 25, 1965 speech:[vi]

> I know you are asking today, "**How long** will it take?" Somebody's asking, "**How long** will racism blind the visions of men, darken their understanding, and drive bright-eyed wisdom from her sacred throne?" Somebody's asking, "**When will** wounded justice, lying prostrate on the streets of Selma and Birmingham and communities all over the South, be lifted from this dust of shame to reign supreme among the children of men?" Somebody's asking, "**When will** the radiant star of hope be plunged against the nocturnal bosom of this lonely night, plucked from weary souls with chains of fear and the manacles of death? **How long** will justice be crucified, and truth bear it?"
>
> I come to say to you this afternoon, however difficult the moment, however frustrating the hour, it will **not be long**, because "truth crushed to earth will rise again."
>
> **How long? Not long,** because "no lie can live forever."
> **How long? Not long**, because "you shall reap what you sow."
> **How long? Not long:** Truth forever on the scaffold, Wrong forever on the throne, Yet that scaffold sways the future,
> and, behind the dim unknown, Standeth God within the shadow,
> Keeping watch above his own.
> **How long? Not long**, because the arc of the moral universe is long, but it

> bends toward justice.
> **How long? Not long**, because Mine eyes have seen the glory of the coming of the Lord...

As God's family we must not accept a position that allows racial reconciliation progress to not be measured, thus allowing the more things change the more they remain the same. We find our success metrics on the issue of racial reconciliation through what God says to us in his holy word (the Gospel) and through an intentional prayer life. Obedience to both is not optional. God's word, yes; our life and work is all about the Gospel. We cannot expect what is take place among Christ followers to be promulgated in the society at large. But we should expect love among all peoples within the body of Christ. We should not only expect it but hold each other accountable for it. We will stop saying, **we have a long way to go** when we embrace God's perfect love. We will stop saying **we have a long way to go** when we hold and are held accountable for being conduits of God's perfect love. We will stop saying **we have a long way to go** when we accept God's making of a diverse humanity of multiple diasporas. We will stop saying **we have a long way to go** when we accept the commission to share the Gospel with all peoples regardless of their skin color. We will stop saying **we have a long way to go** when we acknowledge that we don't know what to do share ministry with others who are different than us; yet when a biblically sound missional framework is presented it is ignored or changed to maintain the status quo.

Complacency in racial reconciliation ministry is not desirable nor acceptable for the Christ follower who walks in the power of the Holy Spirit. Do I love more today than I did yesterday? Am I moving beyond the sins that so easily set me and thus my kingdom work back? God has a plan for every Christian's growth. The plan is not one of procrastination or infinite stagnation. It is one of radical transformation that occurs with all deliberate speed.

Christians are accountable for the Gospel. On the other hand, secular society, all too often, is not accountability to anyone or any community purpose. Separate but equal was unequal historically and is still unequal from every angle because God's Plan A is "together" not separate. In the body of Christ when we are separate, especially in worship, mission, and ministry "the church" misses out. For Christians when the Gospel goes forward, peoples are reconciled, yes even racially reconciled. It is through the Gospel that we are reconciled with God and each other. At this point, it is good to give some time to the foundations of the Gospel as it points to racial reconciliation.[vii]

Chapter 1

Unpacking the Gospel

The Gospel is the fundamental reason we must have the racial reconciliation conversation. The Gospel is to be shared among all peoples and lived out as a testimony within the body of Christ. This sharing is to be through all believers to none believers so that the transforming power of the love of God can be experienced by men, women, boys, and girls of all races. The Gospel is the fundamental reason we must take missional actions of love toward all people. The Gospel is the fundamental reason we must evaluate and measure how we are doing based on a biblical worldview framework. If we want to blame an agitator in the Christian context for not being able to look past racial reconciliation; we must point to the Gospel.

God is the only owner of Gospel.

> [9] In this was manifested the love of God toward us, because that God sent his only begotten Son into the world, that we might live through him. [10] Herein is love, not that we loved God, but that he loved us, and sent his Son *to be* the propitiation for our sins. 1 John 4:9-10

The Gospel is God's Great News for people who have no relationship with him. God is the only authenticator of the Gospel. No person, black or white, is given authority to create a racial or cultural gospel. The Gospel is the heart of God. He so loves us that he sent Jesus to die for our sins. And because the Gospel belongs to God, he is jealously protective of it. He does not want the Gospel mixed with any religious creeds, ordinances, or traditions. He does not want it mixed with any of man's ideologies, theories, or laws. He definitely does not want the Gospel subjugated to any government.

The Gospel is God's pure message to sinful man. The covering has been torn open, and now the glory shines out; and whenever the Gospel is proclaimed, it tells of the way into

God's glorious kingdom for sinful man, the way to come before the Mercy Seat cleaned from every stain. It is the Gospel of the Glory of God, because, until Christ had entered into the Glory, it could not be preached in its fullness, but, after the glory received Him, then the message is now able to go out to a lost world. The Gospel solely belongs to God.

There is only one Gospel.

> [6] I marvel that you are turning away so soon from Him who called you in the grace of Christ, to a different gospel, [7] which is not another; but there are some who trouble you and want to pervert the gospel of Christ. [8] But even if we, or an angel from heaven, preach any other gospel to you than what we have preached to you, let him be accursed. [9] As we have said before, so now I say again, if anyone preaches any other gospel to you than what you have received, let him be accursed. [10] For do I now persuade men, or God? Or do I seek to please men? For if I still pleased men, I would not be a bondservant of Christ. Galatians 1:6-10

> [3] Jesus answered and said unto him, Verily, verily, I say unto thee, except a man be born again, he cannot see the kingdom of God. [4] Nicodemus saith unto him, how can a man be born when he is old? Can he enter the second time into his mother's womb, and be born? [5] Jesus answered, Verily, verily, I say unto thee, except a man be born of water and *of* the Spirit, he cannot enter into the kingdom of God. [6] That which is born of the flesh is flesh; and that which is born of the Spirit is spirit. [7] Marvel not that I said unto thee, ye must be born again. John 3:3-7

The Gospel is not a Gospel; it is the only Gospel. There is not a different gospel for each Diaspora. There is not a white gospel nor a black gospel. Although the pictures that hang in many homes and churches indicate otherwise, there is not a Jesus for Europeans and another Jesus for Africans. Just as there is not a white heaven or a black heaven but one heaven. There are serious questions about professed Christians who discriminately disavow people from the saving power of the Gospel and thus Heaven based on the color of lost person's skin. How do we disavow people, we do so when we don't intentionally share the Gospel with them.

We had nothing to do with our physical birth, and can have nothing to do with our second birth. It must be the work of God, and it permeates the Gospel. Everywhere the Apostles went they preached the Gospel of the Kingdom of God, and they showed that the only way to get into that Kingdom was by a second birth, and that the only way the second birth could happen was through believing the Gospel - the one and only Gospel. It is the Holy Spirit that overcomes the natural unbelief of the human heart and enables a man to put his trust (faith) in the Gospel. And this is not mere intellectual assent, but it is that one comes to the place where he is ready to stake his whole eternity on the fact that Christ died, and was buried, and rose again. So yes the Gospel always goes by the cross but it doesn't stay there.

The Gospel doesn't have an expiration date.

> [23] Being born again, not of corruptible seed, but of incorruptible, by the word of God, which liveth and abideth forever. [24]For all flesh *is* as grass, and all the glory of man as the flower of grass. The grass withereth, and the flower thereof falleth away: [25]But the word of the Lord endureth forever. And this is the word which by the gospel is preached unto you. 1 Peter 1:23-25

The gospel will never be surpassed by another. The Gospel is everlasting. There was no other gospel before it and there is no need to look for another one to come. If this world will be around for billions of years, it will never need another Gospel than the one that is proclaimed by God's word and confirmed with all types of miracles, signs, and wonders throughout history saving innumerable sinners like you and me. There are not seasons to share the Gospel, but the Gospel should flow from believers to all types of non-believers all the time.

The Gospel has a Resurrected Christ.

> [12] Now if Christ be preached that he rose from the dead, how say some among you that there is no resurrection of the dead? [13] But if there be no resurrection of the dead, then is Christ not risen: [14] And if Christ be not risen, then *is* our preaching vain, and your faith *is* also vain. [15] Yea, and we are found false witnesses of God; because we have testified of God that he raised up Christ: whom he raised not up, if so be that the dead rise not. [16] For if the dead rise not, then is not Christ raised: [17] And if Christ be not raised, your faith *is* vain; ye are yet in your sins. [18] Then they also which are fallen asleep in Christ are perished. [19] If in this life only we have hope in Christ, we are of all men most miserable. 1 Corinthians 15:12-19

We rejoice at the love that called our Lord and Savior from his heavenly position to an old rugged cross. Yes, surely he died on Calvary. That in itself is an awesome feat. The perfection in God saw to it that the propitiation for our sins was complete; so our savior is a resurrected Savior. Thank God he was born of a virgin and unjustly crucified as a substitution but we must know and proclaim that he got up. The Gospel is the Gospel of the Resurrected Christ. There would be no Gospel for sinners if Christ had not been raised from the grave. Surely resurrection power trumps racial differences.

The Gospel has a living Christ.

> [21] For after that in the wisdom of God the world by wisdom knew not God, it pleased God by the foolishness of preaching to save them that believe. [22] For the

> Jews require a sign, and the Greeks seek after wisdom: ²³But we preach Christ crucified, unto the Jews a stumbling block, and unto the Greeks foolishness; ²⁴But unto them which are called, both Jews and Greeks, Christ the power of God, and the wisdom of God. 1 Corinthians 1:21-24

> ²⁷ Then saith he to Thomas, Reach hither thy finger, and behold my hands; and reach hither thy hand, and thrust *it* into my side: and be not faithless, but believing. ²⁸And Thomas answered and said unto him, My Lord and my God. ²⁹ Jesus saith unto him, Thomas, because thou hast seen me, thou hast believed: blessed *are* they that have not seen, and *yet* have believed. ³⁰ And many other signs truly did Jesus in the presence of his disciples, which are not written in this book: John 20:27-30

It is not enough that Jesus Christ was resurrected and lived for a time after resurrection. He is alive even until today and will be forevermore. For those who say "The body of Jesus still sleeps in a Middle Eastern tomb, but His soul goes marching on" I say, "that is not the Gospel of Christ". We do not preach the Gospel of a dead Christ, but of a living Christ who sits exalted at the Father's right hand, and is living to save all who put their trust in Him. That is why those of us who really know the Gospel never have any crucifixes around our churches or in our homes. The crucifix represents a dead Christ hanging weak and stiff on a cross of shame. But we are not pointing men to a dead Christ; we are preaching a living Christ. He lives exalted at God's right hand, and He "saves to the uttermost all who come to God by Him."

The Gospel is empowering.

> ¹⁶For I am not ashamed of the gospel of Christ: for it is the power of God unto salvation to everyone that believeth; to the Jew first, and also to the Greek. ¹⁷For

therein is the righteousness of God revealed from faith to faith: as it is written, the just shall live by faith. Romans 1:16-17

Moreover, brethren, I declare to you the gospel which I preached to you, which also you received and in which you stand, [2] by which also you are saved, if you hold fast that word which I preached to you—unless you believed in vain. [3] For I delivered to you first of all that which I also received: that Christ died for our sins according to the Scriptures, [4] and that He was buried, and that He rose again the third day according to the Scriptures. 1 Corinthians 15:1-4

The power for racial reconciliation is found in the Gospel. While secular society can do good things and take positive steps to demonstrate good will, only the transforming power of the Gospel can change hearts.

"The Gospel is Grace Full."

Our reconciliation to God leaves no room for works. All of our pretending goodness is stripped away by the Gospel and we see we deserve nothing. The Gospel is smothered in grace and grace is God's underserved favor to those who deserve the opposite. The Gospel is not one of works. Romans 11:6 and Ephesians 2:9-10 speaks to this:

> [6] And if by grace, then *is it* no more of works: otherwise grace is no more grace. But if *it be* of works, then is it no more grace: otherwise work is no more work. Romans 11:6
> [8] For by grace are ye saved through faith; and that not of yourselves: *it is* the gift of God: [9] Not of works, lest any man should boast.
> Ephesians 2:8-9

> …there was a boatman and two theologians in a boat, and one was arguing that salvation was by faith and the other by works. The boatman listened, and then said, "Let me tell you how it looks to me. Suppose I call this oar Faith and this one Works. If I pull on this one, the boat goes around; if I pull on this other one, it goes around the other way, but if I pull on both oars, I get you across the river." I have heard many preachers use that illustration to prove that we are saved by faith and works. That might do if

> we were going to Heaven in a rowboat, but we are not. We are carried on the shoulders of the Shepherd, who came seeking lost sheep When He finds them He carries them home on His shoulders.[viii]

What about the man who does not believe the Gospel? The Lord Jesus said to His disciples, "Go ye into all the world and preach the Gospel to every creature. He that believeth not shall be judged, and condemned, lost. So you see, God has made the Gospel the only way. I don't want to make assumptions. If you have been resting in anything other than the Christ who died, who was buried, who rose again; turn from it, and run to Christ today. Repent and believe the Gospel. We must pray that the Gospel goes forward in full power.

There will not be significant racial reconciliation without significant embracing of the Gospel. The Gospel is full of grace and so to must we be if are to carry out the ministry of racial reconciliation.

Amazing Grace is probably the most popular hymn in the English language— maybe it is because its words so well describe the author: John Newton was a slave trader before coming to Christ. Isn't it like God that he would use the testimony of a former slave trader to become the traditional musical introduction for the presentation of the Gospel by many black churches being sang just before the preacher stands to proclaim the word of God.

Amazing grace! (How sweet the sound)
That sav'd a wretch like me!
I once was lost, but now am found,
was blind, but now I see.

'Twas grace that taught my heart to fear,
And grace my fears reliev'd;
How precious did that grace appear
The hour I first believ'd!

Thro' many dangers, toils, and snares,
I have already come;
'Tis grace hath brought me safe thus far,
and grace will lead me home.

The Lord has promis'd good to me,
His word my hope secures;
He will my shield and portion be
As long as life endures.

Yes, when this flesh and heart shall fail,
And mortal life shall cease;
I shall possess, within the veil,
A life of joy and peace.

The earth shall soon dissolve like snow,
The sun forbear to shine;
But God, who call'd me here below,
Will be forever mine.

John Newton, *Olney Hymns*, 1779

The Gospel must be shared

> ⁸But what does it say? "The word is near you; it is in your mouth and in your heart," that is, the message concerning faith that we proclaim: ⁹If you declare with your mouth, "Jesus is Lord," and believe in your heart that God raised him from the dead, you will be saved. ¹⁰For it is with your heart that you believe and are justified, and it is with your mouth that you profess your faith and are saved. ¹¹As Scripture says, "Anyone who believes in him will never be put to shame. ¹² For there is no difference between Jew and Gentile—the same Lord is Lord of all and richly blesses all who call on him, ¹³ for, "Everyone who calls on the name of the Lord will be saved. Romans 10:8-13 NIV

The Gospel is intended to be shared, not horded by a limited number of people who feel they have an exclusive privilege of being in the family of God. Just as it is not a difficult thing to understand the Gospel, it is also not as hard as we make it to regularly share our faith, even among people who are different from us. Racial reconciliation includes sharing the Gospel cross racially. This is not an option for a Christ follower. God's word declares he that wins souls is wise. We win souls by sharing the Gospel.

> The fruit of the [uncompromisingly] righteous is a tree of life, and he who is wise captures human lives [for God, as a fisher of men–he gathers and receives them for eternity]. [Matthew 4:19; I Corinthians 9:19; James 5:20.] Behold, the [uncompromisingly] righteous shall be recompensed on earth; how much more the wicked and the sinner! And if the righteous are barely saved, what will become of the ungodly and wicked? I Peter 4:18. and Proverbs 11:30-31

When we share the Gospel we move the society toward looking like the kingdom. Political maneuvering cannot accomplish this. While public policy changes legalities, only the Gospel can transform hearts.

Chapter 2

> He who is devoid of the power to forgive, is devoid of the power to love.   MLK, Jr.

Forgiveness – Don't try to do life without it

Throughout history and even now, people from all over the world have marveled at the general corporate forgiveness demonstrated throughout America's history that has included African (blacks) and Europeans (whites). After hundreds of years of black slavery in America; how can we be so close to being an example of forgiveness? The answer is God, God's word and God's people. The 21st century challenge, as we get ever closer to true kingdom brotherhood, makes us realize the gulf between biblical reconciliation on a forgiveness platform and reconciliation for political or ideological compromise. From all sectors of the world people seek to get handles on relationships that are made up of many components and actions. Right and wrong is always a part of life's equation whether you are an unbeliever, a carnal Christian, or an ever maturing disciple. Forgiveness is difficult and in some cases complex. Forgiveness is mandatory for the Christian. Don't try to do life without it.

Forgive us our debts, as we forgive our debtors. Matthew 6:12

When the disciples asked Jesus to teach them how to pray, he responded with what is commonly known as the Lord's Prayer. Embedded in the language of the prayer is this specific request for forgiveness.

It is evident from the content of the prayer that our Lord meant for us to pray after this manner daily, because it includes a request for this day's daily bread. It is therefore equally plain that Jesus is telling us to confess our sins daily and ask daily for God's forgiveness.

Too often we allow a long time, and many unconfessed sins, to amass before we go to the Lord in prayer. As a result, we begin to feel estranged from God; our guilty conscience then makes it even more difficult to go to him in prayer at all. .It is best to keep "short accounts" with God, going to him regularly with our sin debt and allowing him to wipe it clean. We then more easily go to him for a regular time of confession, communion, and refreshing.

Notice, also, how this daily forgiveness is tied purposefully and inseparably to our own forgiveness of others. Jesus, in effect, couches this prayer in such a way that we must either forgive others completely and daily, or we are cursing ourselves each time we pray!

"Forgive us as we forgive others," Jesus tells us to pray. Have you taken your sin-debt to God in prayer today? Have you forgiven others as you yourself hope to be forgiven?

> Be ye kind one to another, tenderhearted, forgiving one another, even as God for Christ's sake hath forgiven you   Ephesians 4:32

What soft comfort and what hard conviction are contained in this one directive! First, we are told that God has, for Christ's sake, forgiven you (if you are among "the faithful in Christ Jesus" to whom Paul was writing).

Not only has he forgiven you, but he has done so with kindness and with tenderness of heart. This is no begrudging, reluctant forgiveness. God's heart is tender toward us. His love toward us is genuine and his forgiveness is complete.

However, the more we marvel at the undeserved and 'graceful' love of God for us, the more we convict ourselves by the standard that is here set before us. We are to be kind, and tenderhearted, and forgiving toward one another in the same way that God was kind, and tenderhearted, and forgiving toward us.

How did God forgive you? Did he wait until you deserved his forgiveness? Did he make you grovel, or earn, or beg for it? Does he bring your past sins up over and over again in order to shame you? Did he wait for you to pursue him, or did he pursue you in order to bring about healing and reconciliation in your relationship with him?

The overwhelming teaching of Scripture -- and especially the first half of the book of Ephesians -- is that God sought us out and forgave us in Christ without any conditions, or qualifications being met by us. We, therefore, ought to be just as kind, just as tender, just as forgiving toward each other.

> Moreover if thy brother shall trespass against thee, go and tell him his fault between thee and him alone: if he shall hear thee, thou hast gained thy brother. But if he will not hear thee, then take with thee one or two more, that in the mouth of two or three witnesses every word may be established. And if he shall neglect to hear them, tell it unto the church: but if he neglect to hear the church, let him be unto thee as an heathen man and a publican. Then came Peter to him, and said, Lord, how oft shall my brother sin against me, and I forgive him? till seven times? Jesus saith unto him, I say not unto thee, until seven times: but, until seventy times seven. (Matthew 18:15-17, .21-22 KJV

If we are honest with ourselves, Peter's question is one we all would have wanted to ask. Exactly how many times is it necessary to forgive the same person? To Peter, and to our natural reasoning, seven times seems fairly generous.

But Jesus counters with a grudge-shattering, jaw-dropping figure that is in itself clearly intended to end all our attempts to mark and number each other's offenses. Turn the pencil around and erase all the wrongs you have carefully been taking note of. Complete and immediate forgiveness, Jesus says, is still in order.

Sometimes it is not so much the number of wounds as the magnitude of one great injury that makes it difficult to forgive. What about a people that were enslaved by the millions even unnumbered others dying in the middle passage.

As C.S. Lewis observes,

> ... it is necessary to forgive, not just 490 times for 490 offenses, but 490 times for one great and terrible injustice -- every time the sting of it is felt again in your heart.[ix]

As he does in every place the issue arises, Jesus puts to permanent rest any hope of a righteous grudge. If, as Jesus reminds Peter in the parable immediately following this directive, God has forgiven us so much, how can we refuse to forgive those who insult or injure us not only in the past but presently.

If we believe that God forgives us our sins; but also that He will not do so unless we forgive other people their sins against us; there is no doubt about the second part of this statement. It is in the Lord's Prayer, it was emphatically stated by our Lord. If you don't forgive you will not be forgiven. No exceptions to it. He doesn't say that we are to forgive other people's sins, provided they are not too deployable, or provided there are extenuating circumstances, or anything of that sort. We are to forgive them all, however spiteful, however mean, however often they are repeated. If we don't we shall be forgiven none of our own.

Now it seems to me that we often make a mistake both about God's forgiveness of our sins and about the forgiveness we are told to offer to other people's sins. Take it first about God's forgiveness, I find that when I think I am asking God to forgive me I am often in reality (unless I watch myself very carefully) asking Him to do something quite different. I am asking him not to forgive me but to excuse me. But there is all the difference in the world between forgiving and excusing. Forgiveness says, "Yes, you have done this thing, but I accept your apology; I will never hold it against you and everything between us two will be exactly as it was before." If one was not really to blame then there is nothing to forgive. In that sense forgiveness and excusing are almost opposites. Of course, in many cases, either between God and man, or between one man and another, there may be a mixture of the two. Part of what at first seemed to be the sins turns out to be really nobody's fault and is excused; the bit that is left over is forgiven. If you had a perfect excuse, you would not need forgiveness; if the whole of your actions needs forgiveness, then there was no excuse for it. But the trouble is that what we call "asking God's forgiveness" very often really consists in asking God to accept our excuses. What leads us into this mistake is the fact that there usually is some amount of excuse, some "extenuating circumstances." We are so very anxious to point these things out to God (and to ourselves) that we are apt to forget the very important thing; that is, the part left over, the part which excuses don't cover, the bit which is inexcusable but not, thank God, unforgivable. And if we forget this, we go away imagining that we have repented and been forgiven when all that has really happened is that we have satisfied ourselves with our own excuses. They may be very bad excuses; we are all too easily satisfied about ourselves.

There are two remedies for this danger. One is to remember that God knows all the real excuses very much better than we do. If there are real "extenuating circumstances" there is no fear that He will overlook them. God knows many excuses that we have never even thought of, and therefore humble souls will, after death, have the delightful surprise of discovering that on certain occasions they sinned much less than they thought. All the real excusing God will do. What we have got to take to Him is the inexcusable part, **the sin.** We are only wasting our time talking about all the parts which can (we think) be excused. When you go to a Dr. you show him the part of you that is wrong - say, a broken arm. It would be a mere waste of time to keep on explaining that your legs and throat and eyes are all right. You may be mistaken in thinking so, and anyway, if they are really right, the doctor will know that.

The second remedy is really and truly to believe in the forgiveness of sins. A great deal of our anxiety to make excuses comes from not really believing in it, from thinking that God will not take us to Himself again unless He is satisfied that some sort of case can be made out in our favor. But that is not forgiveness at all. Real forgiveness means looking steadily at the sin, the sin that is left over without any excuse, after all allowances have been made, and seeing it in all its horror, dirt, meanness, and malice, and nevertheless being wholly reconciled to the man who has done it.

When it comes to a question of our forgiving other people, it is partly the same and partly different. It is the same because, here also forgiving does not mean excusing. Many people seem to think it does. They think that if you ask them to forgive someone who has cheated or committed racism you are trying to make out that there was really no cheating or racism. But if that were so, there would be nothing to forgive. (This doesn't mean that you must necessarily believe his next promise. It does mean that you must make every effort to kill every taste of resentment in your own heart - every wish to humiliate or hurt him or to pay him back.)

In our own case we accept excuses too easily, in other people's we do not accept them easily enough. As regards my own sins I can say that the excuses are not really as good as I think; as regards other men's sins against me it is a safe assumption (though not a certainty) that the excuses are better than I think. One must therefore begin by attending to everything which may show that the other man was not so much to blame as we thought. But even if he is absolutely fully to blame we still have to forgive him; and even if ninety-nine per cent of his apparent guilt can be explained away by really good excuses, the problem of forgiveness begins with the one per cent of guilt that remains. To excuse, what can really produce good excuses is not Christian love; it is only fairness. **To be a Christian means to forgive the inexcusable, because God has forgiven the inexcusable in you.**

This is hard. It is perhaps not so hard to forgive a single great injury. But to forgive the incessant provocations of daily life - to keep on forgiving the racist jokes, racist employment practices, or even the selfish daughter, the lying son - How can we do it? Only, I think, by remembering where we now live in Jesus Christ, by meaning our words when we say in our prayers each night "Forgive our trespasses" as we forgive those that trespass against us." We are offered forgiveness on no other terms. To refuse it is to refuse God's mercy for ourselves. There is no hint of exceptions to God's word here and God means what He says.

People from whom we need forgiveness

> "For if you forgive men their trespasses, your heavenly Father will also forgive you. But if you do not forgive men their trespasses, neither will your Father forgive your trespasses. (Matthew 6:14-15 NKJV)

One of the largest segments of people from whom we need forgiveness are those family. Friends, co-workers, classmates, neighbors and divine appointments who we did not/have not shared the good news of the Gospel.. May they forgive our disappointing behavior especially at times when it is because they don't look like us.

People to whom we need to offer forgiveness

> As the elect of God...forbearing one another, and forgiving one another, if any man have a quarrel against any: even as Christ forgave you. Colossians 3:12-13

How must God's saints respond to God's gift of salvation to them? How should those who have been themselves forgiven every offense behave, then, towards others?

Paul makes a direct connection between the forgiveness that saints have in Christ and the forgiveness that believers ought to practice themselves. "Even as Christ forgave you," Paul says, you ought to forgive -- with the same unconditional and full forgiveness.

And how broadly does the command apply? If anyone has anything against any one! We cannot claim that anyone is too insignificant, or that any offense is too significant, for us to pardon. This includes matters that are racial, ethnic, or cultural.

Were we not important in relation to God, when he forgave us? Weren't our trespasses against him many and major? And yet God was gracious. Even so, we are told, we are to grant forgiveness wherever we go and with whomever we come in contact.

Are you aware of the extent of God's grace to you? Are you aware of how utterly undeserving you are of his continued forgiveness? If so, then there should be no delay on your part to reflect God's goodness, even to the most unpleasant and abusive of people. Whether this is to a person or people you once hated or who hates you.[x]

The things and occasions for which we need forgiveness from God

If we confess our sins, he is faithful and just to forgive us our sins, and to cleanse us from all unrighteousness. 1 John 1:9

We all need God's forgiveness of sin. It is not a question of if but when we sin. Aren't you thankful for the "all"s and "every"s of the Bible? Because there are so many times that we would be sure to look for a loophole or an exception if God's Word was not so clearly making a universal statement or affirmation. For instance, there are sins which we commit that have consequences the rest of our lives. We are faced daily with reminders of these sins in the past and struggle still with the consequences of many of them. For this reason, we might be tempted to think that such terrible sins cannot be forgiven. How could God forgive me for that?   Can God forgive me for that? Yes he can and he has.

Yet, God's Word gives us this blessed assurance: if we confess our sins, no matter what the sin is; God is faithful to forgive and to cleanse us from all unrighteousness! No sin is exempted. No mistake is too big and no transgression is too heinous for God to cleanse it with the blood of Jesus Christ.

Sanctify them by Your truth. Your word is truth. John 17:17 NKJV

Juneteenth is the oldest known celebration commemorating the ending of slavery in the United States. Dating back to 1865, it was on June 19th that the Union soldiers, led by Major General Gordon Granger, landed at Galveston, Texas with news that the war had ended and that the enslaved were now free. Note that this was two and a half years <u>after</u> President Lincoln's Emancipation Proclamation - which had become official January 1, 1863. The Emancipation Proclamation had little impact on the Texans due to the minimal number of Union troops to enforce the new Executive Order. However, with the surrender of General Lee in April of 1865, and the arrival of General Granger's regiment, the forces were finally strong enough to influence and overcome the resistance.

Later attempts to explain this two and a half year delay in the receipt of this important news have yielded several versions that have been handed down through the years. Often told is the story of a messenger who was murdered on his way to Texas with the news of freedom. Another, is that the news was deliberately withheld by the enslavers to maintain the labor force on the plantations. And still another, is that federal troops actually waited for the slave owners to reap the benefits of one last cotton harvest before going to Texas to enforce the Emancipation Proclamation. All of which, or neither of these version could be true. Certainly, for some, President Lincoln's authority over the rebellious states was in question. Whatever the reasons, conditions in Texas remained status quo well beyond what was statutory. [xi]

Delay is not denial and dreaming is not demonstration. I will not be denied and I will demonstrate the marvelous work God has done in me through Jesus Christ my Lord and Savior. Thank God for what American government did in 1863; but there are some things I have access to through God's forgiveness toward me and my forgiveness from and toward others. Through this access I can chose.

I chose to be free

> Then Jesus said to those Jews who believed Him, "If you abide in My word, you are My disciples indeed. And you shall know the truth, and the truth shall make you free." John 8:31-32 NKJV

I chose to forgive

"For if you forgive men their trespasses, your heavenly Father will also forgive you. But if you do not forgive men their trespasses, neither will your Father forgive your trespasses.   Matthew 6:14-15 NKJV

I chose peace

Be anxious for nothing, but in everything by prayer and supplication, with thanksgiving, let your requests be made known to God; and the peace of God, which surpasses all understanding, will guard your hearts and minds through Christ Jesus. Philippians 4:6-7 NKJV

I chose joy

"These things I have spoken to you, that My joy may remain in you, and that your joy may be full. This is My commandment, that you love one another as I have loved you. John 15:11-12 NKJV

I chose to love

And now abide faith, hope, love, these three; but the greatest of these is love. I Corinthians 13:13 NKJV

Chapter 3

Understanding Racial Reconciliation

Reconciliation is not found in ideology. Ideology causes well-meaning Christians to join in with political agendas and not live out the word of God. Reconciliation is only arrived at through convergent journeys toward a Biblical worldview in the power of transformed hearts. We reconcile with God through embracing a Biblical worldview. We reconciling with other believers especially those who are different in love that only the power of the Holy Spirit can exude. We reconcile our desires with the mission of God and the realities of the mission field as we walk in our calling. Important to our work in God's mission is to know that there will not be revival and spiritual awakening in the land without extensive reconciliation.

For the Christian disciple, we are in the same family and we have a common enemy. We must be all in. Our actions should reflect our oneness in Christ. We must live out the word of God not political ideology or dogma. Being democrat or republican is not a prerequisite for Christian discipleship. In fact through my lens, political voting has been an optional challenge for my voting life as neither major party and most candidates do not operate from a biblical worldview. I am saying let's not start with political conversations. Maybe we should never get to them. Currently even in the body of Christ our actions are challenged by the words of Martin Luther King, Jr. – "We must learn to live together as brothers or we will perish as fools."[xii] Forgiveness is not only the bedrock of our reconciliation with God but with each other.

> Lord, how oft shall my brother sin against me, and I forgive him? Till seven times? Jesus saith unto him, I say not unto thee, Until seven times: but, Until seventy times seven- Matthew 18:21-22

As evangelicals we embrace our salvation as a miraculous transformation from an old life to a new life in Christ. There is not a different salvation for different ethnic groups. We are one in the body of Christ. We then begin a progressive transformational process of becoming more and more like Jesus Christ. All three persons of the God Head trinity play a part in the disciple's salvation and journey toward eternity. The person of the Holy Spirit is active and his ministry within the body of Christ must be received.

God is all about love. Whether speaking about our Christianity, other religions, and even if we ascribe to no religion at all it does not change who God is and what he is about. Most especially for Christians, where there is love, there is trust in the fox holes when we are on the battlefield for the Lord. Let's acknowledge that for some 400 years Christians have not assertively spoken to the issue of race relations in the context of America. Why? From our earliest American history to when the Sunday bells ring in 21st century America we still go to our even more separate corners to worship "our" God who is 'LOVE.' (John 3:16) Continuing this weekly demonstration says to those outside of the family of God that separation in the body of Christ is a necessary and good thing. We are separate on Sundays because we do life apart the rest of the week.[xiii]

In the 20st century, America as a nation stepped up to legislative, judicial, and executive change. This is what those largely outside of the body of Christ specialize in. These 20th century changes all played a part in changing laws and guidelines but do very little if anything to change hearts. As Martin Luther King Jr. reflects even these legal changes happened in spite of little support from the white evangelical Christian community. Martin Luther's King Jr.'s "Letter from a Birmingham Jail" in 1963 is a familiar documentation of this time of history.

> MY DEAR FELLOW CLERGYMEN:
>
> While confined here in the Birmingham city jail, I came across your recent statement calling my present activities "unwise and untimely." ... You deplore the demonstrations taking place in Birmingham. But your statement, I am sorry to say, fails to express a similar concern for the conditions that brought about the demonstrations. I am sure that none of you would want to rest content with the superficial kind of social analysis that deals merely with effects and does not grapple with underlying causes... Let me take note of my other major disappointment. I have been so greatly disappointed with the white church and its leadership. Of course, there are some notable exceptions. I am not unmindful of the fact that each of you has taken some significant stands on this issue. I commend you, Reverend Stallings, for your Christian stand on this past Sunday, in welcoming Negroes to your worship service on a non-segregated basis. I commend the Catholic leaders of this state for integrating Spring Hill College several years ago.
>
> But despite these notable exceptions, I must honestly reiterate that I have been disappointed with the church. I do not say this as one of those negative critics who can always find something wrong with the church. I say this as a minister of the gospel, who loves the church; who was nurtured in its bosom; who has been sustained by its spiritual blessings and who will remain true to it...[xiv]

Can we recognize the needed 21st century heart change is different from passing laws and litigation? Even more can we acknowledge that only God can transform hearts? Among Christians those who are not afraid of holiness, the Holy Spirit, and transformation in community embrace Malachi 3:16 and Acts 2:46-47.

> [16] Then they that feared the LORD spake often one to another: and the LORD hearkened, and heard *it*, and a book of remembrance was written before him for them that feared the LORD, and that thought upon his name. (Malachi 3:16 NKJV)
>
> [46]So continuing daily with one accord in the temple, and breaking bread from house to house, they ate their food with gladness and simplicity of heart,

> praising God and having favor with all the people. ⁴⁷And the Lord added to the church daily those who being saved. (Acts 2:46-47 NKJV)

Unfortunately, we have learned to talk at each other and not to each other, especially across racial lines.[xv] Assumptive behavior statements cannot justify ungodly actions much less help progress in racial reconciliation. Examples of assumptive behavior statements are when it is said "older white men are racist so why reach out to them?" or "young black men are killing each other so why shouldn't the police kill them?" or if they call themselves the "N word" why shouldn't I call them the same? We engage in assumptive behavior statements when our actions declare no distinction between disciples of a racial group and non-disciples of a racial group. We become one in Christ even with our physical differences.

God is not color blind. Since he never makes a mistake we must accept that God is very intentional about racial diversity. In this intent, there is not even the hint of supremacy of one race above another within the body of Christ or outside it. As we strive to be like God, the goal much less the declaration, "that one is color blind" is not a Godly goal or aspiration. If we can have our eyes open and say we do not see color, we also do not see the need to speak to wrongs resulting from the lack of reconciliation. If we close our eyes and say we do not see color; we join the deafening silence of not being reconciled. We must open our eyes. We should see race, but we should strive to a point where race does not matter.

In the 21st century can we be so bold as to speak against one people asserting themselves over another. There are still those who seek to theologically assert some form of supremacy. What makes God angry should make us angry. As brought out in the book of Numbers, the sin of racism is to be taken seriously.

> 1 And Miriam and Aaron spake against Moses because of the Ethiopian woman whom he had married: for he had married an Ethiopian woman. 2 And they said, hath the LORD indeed spoken only by Moses? Hath he not spoken also by us? And the LORD heard it. 3 (Now the man Moses was very meek, above all the men which were upon the face of the earth.) 4 And the LORD spake suddenly unto Moses, and unto Aaron, and unto Miriam, Come out ye three unto the tabernacle of the congregation. And they three came out. 5And the LORD came down in the pillar of the cloud, and stood in the door of the tabernacle, and called Aaron and Miriam: and they both came forth. 6 And he said, Hear now my words: If there be a prophet among you, I the LORD will make myself known unto him in a vision, and will speak unto him in a dream. 7My servant Moses is not so, who is faithful in all mine house. 8 With him will I speak mouth to mouth, even apparently, and not in dark speeches; and the similitude of the LORD shall he behold: wherefore then were ye not afraid to speak against my servant Moses? 9 And the anger of the LORD was kindled against them; and he departed. 10 And the cloud departed from off the tabernacle; and, behold, Miriam became leprous, white as snow: and Aaron looked upon Miriam, and, behold, she was leprous. Numbers 12:1-10

There is much being wrongly said about racial reconciliation in some circles these days. Some even feel they can have the conversation only within a certain group or ideology. Can we talk about diversity only within gatherings of black people or solely within so called "solid" or "sharp" evangelical Christians? No guessing needed here, there is not an equal sign between Christianity and racial isolation or political conservatism. The body of Christ is not to be an exclusive club of clones. The one thing that should be the same about those in the body of Christ should be that we are like the biblical Christ at some level and are more like him as the days go by. Just as I should not have to regularly say that I am not a murderer, I should also be secure in not having to regularly verbalize that I am not a racist. We should rather say regularly who we are, we are reconciled lovers of the brothers and sisters of all mothers.

Reconciliation in a biblical perspective is neither liberal nor conservative. Reconciliation is radical as it represents the transformation work of the God head trinity. God loves us as we were/are, but he loves us too much to leave us there. As he works on us we are radically changed. Changed to love. Changed to care. Changed to give. Changed to do good. Changed to walk in integrity. Changed to be bold and courageous in truth. Reconciliation builds community with God, within the family of God, and on the mission field at all levels while transformation takes place.

Reconciliation builds community with God.

> [12] We are not commending ourselves to you again, but giving you an opportunity to be proud of us, so that you may have a reply for those who take pride in the outward appearance rather than in the heart. [13] For if we are out of our mind, it is for God; if we have a sound mind, it is for you. [14] For Christ's love compels us, since we have reached this conclusion: If One died for all, then all died. [15] And He died for all so that those who live should no longer live for themselves, but for the One who died for them and was raised. [16] From now on, then, we do not know anyone in a purely human way. Even if we have known Christ in a purely human way, yet now we no longer know [Him in this way]. [17] Therefore, if anyone is in Christ, [he is] a new creation; old things have passed away, and look, new things have come. [18] Everything is from God, who reconciled us to Himself through Christ and gave us the ministry of reconciliation: [19] That is, in Christ, God was reconciling the world to Himself, not counting their trespasses against them, and He has committed the message of reconciliation to us. [20] Therefore, we are ambassadors for Christ, certain that God is appealing through us. We plead on Christ's behalf, "Be reconciled to God." [21] He made the One who did not know sin to be sin for us, so that we might become the righteousness of God in Him. 2 Corinthians 5:12-21 (HCSB)

We should be constantly reminded that reconciliation starts with regeneration. When we are right with God we will simultaneously become right with man. So we as Christian disciples are God's ambassadors. We grow in our being ambassadors as we grow in the fruit of the spirit.

We must not see others from merely a human point of view. We must evaluate others from God's point of view. What is God's Point of view – all are equal at the Cross. We must come clean in this. This is a radical change from the prevailing American view even among many Christians. We can only thrive in God's point of view if we abide in Christ.

God has given us the ministry of reconciliation and all of us are called to be reconcilers. We must get involved in the hard issues of life. This issues include biblical marriage, life and religious liberty to be sure. Even more the list must never exclude reconciliation. It is not a question to be answered. Can we all get along? It is a command to be carried out. Love your neighbor as yourself. We cannot expect revival in North America without reconciliation. We must address the challenges of doing the ministry of reconciliation through collaborative work. Discipleship really does have its responsibilities. Reconciliation among the peoples who become disciples is such an important part of the Kingdom work that Jesus prayed for it and God's word declares it necessary for a lost world to believe.

> [20]Neither pray I for these alone, but for them also which shall believe on me through their word; [21]That they all may be one; as thou, Father, *art* in me, and I in thee, that they also may be one in us: that the world may believe that thou hast sent me. John 17:20-21 (KJV)

Sunday morning is the most separated hour of the week, not the most segregated time of the week. Not only is this true now, it has been since the earliest times of American slavery. Sunday is a separated time because during all the other days of the week, as much as is in our control, we are segregated. In 2014 surveys reported in the USA today newspaper; 75% (3 out of every 4) white Americans had no black friends and 65% (2 out of every 3) black Americans had no white friends. Intentionally coming together to pray, break bread, fellowship, and gather a better understanding is necessary. The challenge is more than just doing church together; it is about doing life together.

Reconciliation builds community within the Kingdom family.

While the world may speak synonymously about race relations and racial reconciliation. The body of Christ cannot approach biblical racial reconciliation from a tolerance perspective nor one of simply relating to people because it is a good or right thing to do. Toleration feeds stagnation. Biblical racial reconciliation that builds authentic love and community is based on an interdependent love for others beyond racial and ethnic differences. Biblical racial reconciliation feeds kingdom impact.

> [7] Don't be deceived: God is not mocked. For whatever a man sows he will also reap, [8] because the one who sows to his flesh will reap corruption from the flesh, but the one who sows to the Spirit will reap eternal life from the Spirit. [9] So we must not get tired of doing good, for we will reap at the proper time if we don't give up. [10] Therefore, as we have opportunity, we must work for the good of all, especially for those who belong to the household of faith. Galatians 6:7-10 (HCSB**)**

In Genesis chapters 37-50 we find the long account of Joseph. In his life's journey he was thrown in a pit and sold into slavery, both by his brothers. He was further falsely accused, and unjustly put into prison before God lifted him as a ruler in Egypt and used him to save many people during a time of famine. In the latter Genesis chapters (45-50) Joseph fully reveals himself to his brothers, forgives them, and promises to care for them in one of the greatest reconciliation stories of all time.

God intends for us to carry out his kingdom work interdependently and collaboratively not independently and in isolation. Oneness in the body of Christ is not the same as "separate but equal." The more separate we are in the body and in our kingdom work the less we accomplish for the Kingdom and give a strong picture of God's kingdom to a needy dying world.

> "No man is an island, entire of itself; every man is a piece of the continent, a part of the main; if a clod be washed away by the sea, Europe is the less, as well as if a Promontorie were, as well as if a mannor of thy friends or of thine own were; any man's death diminishes me, because I am involved in mankind; And therefore never send to know for whom the bell tolls; It tolls for thee...."[xvi]

There is no disputing that sinful institution of slavery happened and is a significant part of American and Canadian history. Just as Joseph recognizes and was reconciled to his brothers who were responsible for his enslavement so must African Americans be reconciled with those who sold our ancestors into slavery and those who received and used them as slaves. Yes I am saying there are two parts to the slavery reconciliation issue. One is the historical reconciliation within the African Diaspora of brothers and sisters in America with those from Africa. The other is the historical and ongoing need for reconciliation between the African and European Diasporas in North America. This could be one of the most beautiful corporate reconciliation stories of all time. Can we do it? Yes! Within the construct of the body of Christ. Will we do it? The challenge still lays before us. We have a long way to go. **A long way to go is a starting point. It's not a maintenance point.** Do I love more today than I did yesterday... Am I beyond the sin or sins that so easily beset me?

God has a plan for all of our growth so that we don't get stagnated. Complacency is not acceptable nor possible in Christ. We are either moving forward or moving backwards. Progressive sanctification will not allow us to be static in our progress. Love will not allow us to constantly hold back the reins of a unified body of Christ through racial reconciliation.

Reconciliation builds community at all levels of the transformed mission field.

> [10]This is how God's children—and the Devil's children—are made evident. Whoever does not do what is right is not of God, especially the one who does not love his brother. [11] For this is the message you have heard from the beginning: We should love one another, [12] unlike Cain, who was of the evil one and murdered his brother. And why did he murder him? Because his works were evil, and his brothers were righteous. [13] Do not be surprised, brothers, if the world hates you. [14] We know that we have passed from death to life because we love our brothers. The one who does not love remains in death. [15] Everyone who hates his brother is a murderer, and you know that no murderer has eternal life residing in him. [16] This is how we have come to know love: He laid down His life for us. We should also lay down our lives for our brothers. [17] If anyone has this world's goods and sees his brother in need but closes his

> eyes to his [need]—how can God's love reside in him? ¹⁸ Little children, we must not love with word or speech, but with truth and action. ¹⁹ This is how we will know we belong to the truth and will convince our conscience in His presence, ²⁰ even if our conscience condemns us that God is greater than our conscience, and He knows all things. ²¹ Dear friends, if our conscience doesn't condemn [us], we have confidence before God ²² and can receive whatever we ask from Him because we keep His commands and do what is pleasing in His sight. ²³ Now this is His command: that we believe in the name of His Son Jesus Christ, and love one another as He commanded us. ²⁴ The one who keeps His commands remains in Him, and He in him. And the way we know that He remains in us is from the Spirit He has given us. 1 John 3:10-24 (HCSB)

Maybe an even more challenging issue within American Christianity is the notion that if we don't know (pretend not to know) or even ignore an issue it will go away. I have observed this on the individual and corporate levels. Using ignorance to justify silence is no excuse. On the issue of racial reconciliation claiming ignorance has never been a legitimate excuse. Even worse than real ignorance is the pretense of it to exclude speaking truth to the powers that be. We can only move forward in racial reconciliation with Holy Spirit endowed courage. Holy Spirit endowed courage is not intimidated by maintaining financial stability or even physical death.

The Importance of history in racial reconciliation

From this seat history matters and how we present history matters even more. We cannot continue in the existing myopic views of Christian history. Intentionally or unintentionally, we have been/are limited in attempts at having an inclusive view of Christian history. If a part of the Christian family is not involved in the history books and conversations of the Christian movement (academic and other regular presentations) no confidence of being involved in the present work nor the vision of the future can be expected. This sets up a friction that can be used by the devil to deepen other divides. A significant piece of the reconciliation framework within the body of Christ has to include the historical Christian journeys of the various Diasporas.

We must aggressively work toward an inclusionary Christian history presentation even as the whole counsel of God's word is inclusionary. We need to talk about what inclusionary history looks like. Inclusionary history and revisionary history are not the same. Revisionary history has and does take place when the past is presented to obscure what really happened. Inclusionary history does need to place historical facts up to now left out in their rightful place. Too few Christians, white and black even those who are highly educated, know of non-white historical Christian figures. When we more fully embrace an inclusionary Christian history, we will be moving further down the road to racial reconciliation. The table that follows is an example of how we might inform some of this conversation.

For Every _____ of the Faith:	Of the European Diaspora	Of the African Diaspora
Creative Preacher and Writer	John Bunyan[xvii] 1628-1688	Richard Allen[xviii] 1760-1831
International Missionary (Male)	James Hudson Taylor[xix] 1832 – 1905	George Liele[xx], Liele, or Leile, or *George Sharp* 1750–1820
Prophetic Missionary (Male)	Jonathan Edwards[xxi] 1703-1758	Lott Carey[xxii] 1780 – 1828
Home Missionary (Female)	Annie Armstrong[xxiii] 1850-1938	Sojourner Truth[xxiv] 1797-1883
International Missionary (Female)	Lottie Moon[xxv] (Charlotte Digges) 1840-1912	Dr. Louise Fleming[xxvi] 1862-1899
Influential Pastor	Robert G. Lee[xxvii] 1886-1978	C.L. Franklin[xxviii] 1915-1984
Influential Christian Leader	Hershel Hobbs[xxix] 1907-1995	William H. Brewster[xxx] 1897-1987
Transformation Agent	Dietrich Bonhoeffer[xxxi] 1906-1945	Martin Luther King Jr.[xxxii] 1929-1968
Dean of American Preachers	Adrian Rogers[xxxiii] 1931-2005	Garner C. Taylor[xxxiv] 1918-Present
Evangelism and Preaching	Billy Graham[xxxv] 1918-Present	E.K. Bailey[xxxvi] 1945-2003
Renown Gospel Singer and Song Writer	William "Bill" Gaither[xxxvii] 1936-Present	Andrae Crouch[xxxviii] 1942-2015
National Influence Pentecostal	Rod Parsley[xxxix] 1957-Present	T.D. Jakes[xl] 1957-Present
National Influence Pastor/Preacher	David Jeremiah[xli] 1941-Present	Fred Luter[xlii] 1956-Present
Mega Church Leader	Joel Osteen[xliii] 1963-Present	A.R. Barnard[xliv] 1953-Present

Chapter 4

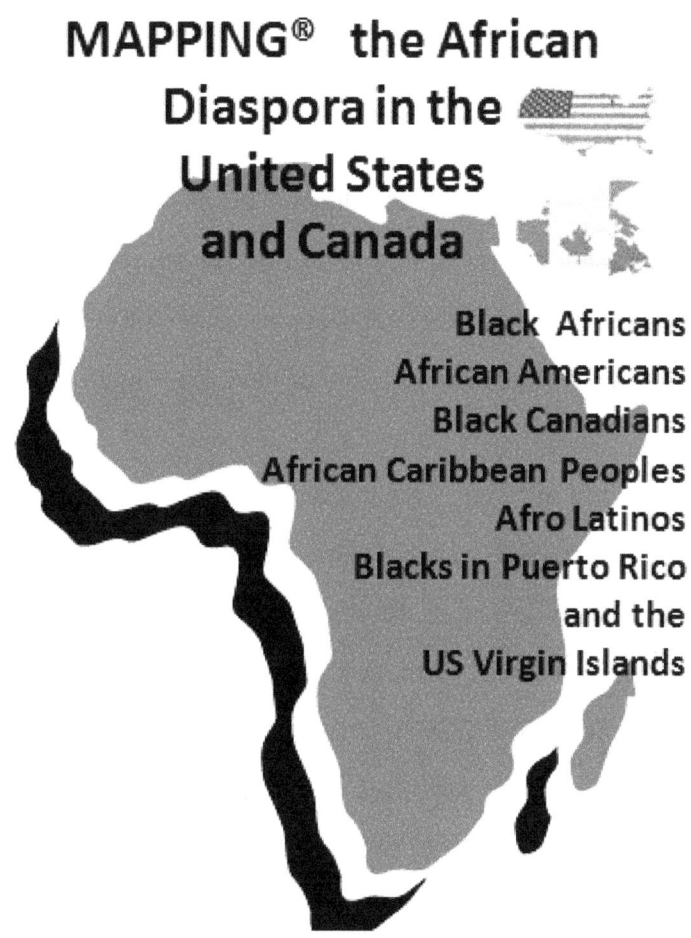

Information Reconciliation and the African Diaspora

What is information reconciliation? It is not drawing a circle around the truth for establishing some cultural or racial empowerment. It is not revisionist history for the convenience of preserving some false notion of people who may have pretended to be reconciled to God and man. Information reconciliation is a process of putting facts together to arrive at the truth. Information reconciliation is important in that along with God's Word and prayer it should inform our missiology. Two significant drivers of the truth are historical realities and current realities. Too many of us (Christians) can't handle the truth. The truth is we are living in and will be for some time in a time of multiple streams of worldviews within races of peoples that the major Diasporas contain. Individuals, especially in America, can no longer have their worldview determined by the color of their skin.

For over 20 years of my ministry, I have used an approach to missional research and analysis that is best described by what I have embraced as **M.A.P.P.I.N.G** (**M**issional **A**nalysis of **P**eoples, **P**laces, **I**nterests, **N**eeds, and **G**odliness) ® based on scriptures found in Numbers 13. MAPPING forces us to look at stubborn facts in the context of a Biblical worldview while desiring to join God in carrying out "his mission." By using the insights of people, experiences, printed and electronic resources, as well as public and private demographics pretty clear patterns of the African Diaspora emerge. The major thesis of what it means to be Black in North America and any further assertions I make about the African Diaspora in the United States and Canada are based on this process.

M.A.P.P.I.N.G. ® A Biblical Foundation

A kingdom movement (or segment of a movement) at any level can only be quantified by an accurate depiction of the starting point. In analysis we show to what extent we accept reality and set a preferred future. You will only know if you are having impact if you pointed to a reality when starting. It is quite telling when the same number of lost figures are used over decades of quantification, in some cases as a badge of honor. Data is unrelentingly stubborn and when faced head on cannot be manipulated.

> Then Moses sent them to spy out the land of Canaan, and said to them, "Go up this *way* into the South, and go up to the mountains, [18] and see what the land is like: whether the people who dwell in it *are* strong or weak, few or many; [19] whether the land they dwell in *is* good or bad; whether the cities they inhabit *are* like camps or strongholds; [20] whether the land *is* rich or poor; and whether there are forests there or not. Numbers 13:17-20 (NKJV)

Verse 17 – A research assignment is given.

- The Focus area (Land of Canaan) is defined.
- Markers identified (From the valley to the mountain)

Verse 18 – Geographic lay-out (natural barriers) to be examined.

Identify the people (Demographic, psychographic and worldview studies)

Verse 19 – How are the cities (places) set up? (Large dense areas or sparse areas)

Are the communities' single or multi-family housing? Gated?

Verse 20 – What is the economy like? Is the area self –propagating? Is there agriculture?

Timber? Indicators of how the people build structures.

Fruit? Crops? Indicators of how the people eat (fellowship).

> Then they told him, and said: "We went to the land where you sent us. It truly flows with milk and honey, and this *is* its fruit. [28] Nevertheless the people who dwell in the land *are* strong; the cities *are* fortified *and* very large; moreover we saw the descendants of Anak there. [29] The Amalekites dwell in the land of the

South; the Hittites, the Jebusites, and the Amorites dwell in the mountains; and the Canaanites dwell by the sea and along the banks of the Jordan." ³⁰ Then Caleb quieted the people before Moses, and said, "Let us go up at once and take possession, for we are well able to overcome it."   Numbers 13:27-30 (NKJV)

Verse 27 – Connecting report with area assigned.

- Verify some assumptions…. Dispel others….
- Wealth and poverty of the area identified
- Visual evidence of what is being reported.

Verse 28 – Profile of the neighborhoods/communities that make up the area.

Profile of the people (s) that stand out or are familiar.

Verse 29 – Initial broad identification of the Peoples. Insight into history and world-view of current residents.

Verse 30 – Immediate response to MAPPING.

Caleb's sense of urgency and purpose.

While we should seek to understand who people say they are; it should not be a practice among Christians to tell peoples who they are racially.[xlv] God did not make a mistake when he made the various peoples of the various Diasporas. He does not make us uniquely different to set one segment of people above another. No matter the Diaspora all are precious in God's sight. No ethnic, racial, or cultural group in America is monolithic (All the same). We must embrace a self-identification paradigm for those who are part of the African Diaspora.

> The word Diaspora is from the Greek διασπορά, "scattering, dispersion. " The dispersion and spreading of a people having a common origin. Such as the African,

Asian, or Latino Diasporas. From the word "diaspeirein" Latin for disperse, and the word "Dia - + speirein" Greek for scatter or sow and from the word "spora" Greek for sowing or reproduction and spreading. For purposes of this paper, this is the accepted definition.

More broadly, the African Diaspora comprises the indigenous, or black peoples of Africa and their descendants, wherever they are in the world beyond the African continent. Pan-Africanists and Afrocentrists often also consider other Negroid (or "Africoid") and Australoid (also called "Veddoid") peoples as diasporic "African peoples." These groups include Tamils (also called Dravidians) and the black, aboriginal peoples of Australia, Melanesia, Polynesia and New Guinea, as well as the Negritos of Southeast Asia (Thailand, Java, Borneo, Sumatra and Malaysia).

The African Diaspora is the Diaspora created by the movements and culture of Africans and their descendants throughout the world, in places including Europe, the Caribbean, North America including the United States and Canada, South America, and Central America. The majority of the African Diaspora are descended from people taken into slavery, but in recent years they include a rising number of voluntary immigrants, emigrants and asylum-seekers as well.

Depending on which estimate is used, it is estimated that between 10 and 25 Million Africans perished in the middle passage. We won't know until Glory. The African peoples transported to the Americas between 1540 and 1850 represent possibly the largest emigration in the history of the world.

It is estimated that of the Africans brought to the new world as slaves, approximately 500,000-700,000 of them came to the United States. This was only about 4 to 6 percent of all who were shipped to the Americas. The majority, about 35% were sent to Brazil. The largest ports of entry for American slaves were Baltimore, Savannah, Charleston and New Orleans.

People of the African Diaspora have a long rich history in the religious, economic, political and social landscape of the United States and Canada. It is important to recognize that the African Diaspora is much broader than the traditionally recognized view of who African Americans are. African Diaspora people are not monolithic and represent a broad array of social, cultural, educational, financial, political, and religious ways of thinking that inform the diverse world views of the North American mission field.

Sociologists separate those within the African Diaspora to make social arguments. Demographers separate those within the African Diaspora to strengthen racial and ethnic divides. In some cases to even validate population theories. Education and religion has separated the African Diaspora due to misinformed research. At the end of the day, the dots of the African Diaspora have somehow remained connected and those who have roots from Africa, although scattered, around the world including North America know we have more in common than we have differences.

Why are people of the African Diaspora Undercounted in America and Canada?
- Immigrants aspiring citizenship in America who are trying to blend in.
- Confusion over how census information will be used so just don't participate.
- Confusion on questions of race and ancestry by those who do respond to census surveys.
- Unclear presentations of various peoples within the African Diaspora by the Census Bureau and other research entities.
- Neighborhoods and Communities where Census counts not verified because of fears of violence by those working as census takers.
- Fear of legal repercussions among Blacks for everything from unpaid parking tickets to more serious arrest warrants.
- Fear of losing government benefits among those who have a living arrangement outside of marriage.

There is much to consider in making disciples through planting the Gospel among those of the African Diaspora in North America. The African Diaspora in America is perhaps more fused than any other Diaspora because of the historical and current realities of race within our borders. We have many worldviews, but we are one people! There is much to celebrate but also much kingdom work to be done.

When we speak of the African Diaspora, it raises some major issues in regard to those known as Black or of African descent within the United States and Canada. 1) There are presently 1 Million plus Canadian immigrants who have African origins directly or through the Caribbean. The 2016 Canadian census when completed will verify this population size. 2) Foreign born Africans and Pan Africans are coming to North America in record numbers and are not being substantially addressed in ministry strategies. In particular, Africans are also coming to the United States in the greatest numbers since slave trading. 3) No other Diaspora is as sub-divided as that of the African Diaspora.

In too many academic and missiological circles, African Americans are not referred to as 4th, 5th or 6th generation Africans and foreign born Africans are most often not demographically connected to African Americans. Other diaspora ethnic groups are most often referenced by generational identification. Race and ethnicity has mattered and continues to matter. Even in foundational demographics the African Diaspora is a divided mosaic whose dots must be connected.

Peoples of the African Diaspora melt into an African-American status when they assimilate into American culture including English language proficiency. But they do not lose their African orientation and connections. Not all Black people assimilate within the same time table. They also don't assimilate to the same levels; hence, the importance of the "African-American" category pointing back to the motherland but acknowledging a new location. It is not new that there are many worldviews within those of the African Diaspora in America. As the rest of American society, Black American worldviews are varied. Race alone does not determine worldview, while the case of its cultural impact can be made.

Serena Williams, at this writing, is the number one women's tennis player in the world. It was interesting to watch the 2013 French Open Women's tennis championship held in Paris, France and observe how America's urban fusion took center stage. The championship match was between Serena Williams a Black American who grew up in an inner city of Los Angeles, California (Compton) and Maria Sharapova, a Russian American who became a naturalized American after achieving success, playing in front of a predominantly French audience. Serena Williams won the match against her number two ranked competitor. In speeches after the tennis match the Russian American who now calls New York City home spoke fluently in English, while the Black American chose to speak fluently in French. New Americans and even aspiring Americans are increasing multi-lingual including fluent English.[xlvi] Neither the European Diaspora nor the African Diaspora is monolithic.

In the broader context, there are really just two types of people. One type is the person on their way to heaven and should have a biblical worldview; and the other is the person who is on their way to hell who can have any number of worldviews. A sinners job description is to sin. A saint's job description is to make disciples while loving like our heavenly brother loved and loves. In the body of Christ, this love cannot be limited to people who are just like us.

The appendix to this book has the most current information regarding the African Diaspora in the United States and Canada. This type of information is important if we are to have racial reconciliation conversations based on empirical facts and not anecdotal statements or assumptions. I acknowledge the complexity of the needed demographic and psychographic conversations in 21st century urban fused America.

Chapter 5

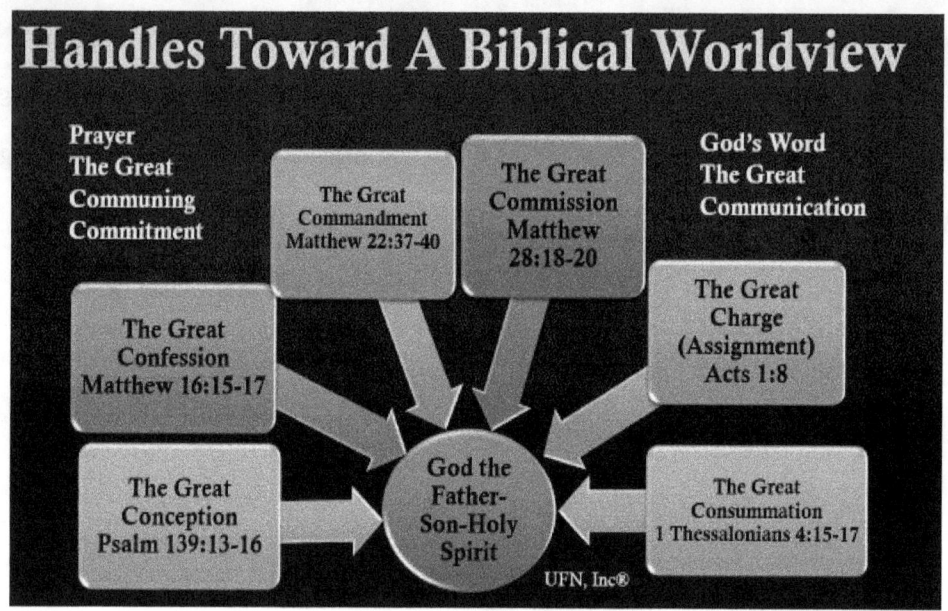

The Necessity of a Biblical worldview[xlvii]

What should make the Christian different from a non-Christian is that the Christian is journeying through life with an ever strengthening biblical worldview. Embracing a Biblical worldview settles many questions before the questions are asked. Racism is rebuffed from every angle of a biblical worldview. Racial reconciliation is fully affirmed by every handle of a biblical worldview. The Christian walk and thus our communities of faith look different from secular groups and other religions when we are shaped by a biblical worldview.

I have arrived at a place where I define a biblical worldview as an overall way of looking at the world based on God's word and Godly revelation as he directs our life on mission with him in the world. This definition does not give me a license to place or blame non-biblical ideology on God. As a disciple I should strive to apply God's word of truth to every aspect of who I am as I am being reconciled in him and my fellow man. The fruit of the spirit is a good indicator of moving toward and operating in a biblical worldview.

All too often we take the holy bible and the one mission of our one God and then we separate into various views on what it all means until our impact is the lowest common Christian denominator. There is plenty of theological leg room as we seek obedience. The part we should focus most on is how we do the mission together.

The next few pages frame what I see as some critical handles of a disciple's biblical worldview. We need to take a fresh look at these timeless Biblical truths in light of the need for reconciliation in the body of Christ.

The Trinity

> ²⁶ And God said, **Let us make man in our image, after our likeness**: and let them have dominion over the fish of the sea, and over the fowl of the air, and over the cattle, and over all the earth, and over every creeping thing that creepeth upon the earth. ²⁷So God created man in his *own* image, in the image of God created he him; male and female created he them. Genesis 1:26-27

A relevant question as I read Genesis 1:26-27 is who is talking to whom? God is not speaking in some human vernacular. God the Father, God the Son and God the Holy Spirit are present and in agreement at creation.

> ¹⁴ The grace of the Lord Jesus Christ, and the love of God, and the communion of the Holy Ghost, *be* with you all. Amen. 2 Corinthians 13:14

This verse not only names each person of the God Head trinity but shares what their unique roles are. The God Head is three distinct persons yet functions as one. The son and the Holy Spirit are not after thoughts that appear on the scene at various points in history. God the Father Son and Holy Spirit have been there all the time. Not just provision for our salvation but our completed salvation rest in God. Because of God's love, we got Jesus. It was the grace of the Lord Jesus that took him through the cross experience as he paid the price for our sins. It is through communion with the Holy Spirit, that he transforms our heart and gives us love and hope here and now.

> ²³**Jesus said to him in answer, if anyone has love for me, he will keep my words: and he will be dear to my Father; and we will come to him and make our living-place with him.** ²⁴ He who has no love for me does not keep my words; and the word which you are hearing is not my word but the Father's who sent me. ²⁵ I have

said all this to you while I am still with you. ²⁶ But the Helper, the Holy Spirit, whom the Father will send in my name, will be your teacher in all things and will put you in mind of everything I have said to you.   (John 14:23-26 BBE)

The Great Conception

¹³ For You formed my inward parts; You covered me in my mother's womb.¹⁴ I will praise You, for I am fearfully *and* wonderfully made; Marvelous are Your works, And *that* my soul knows very well. ¹⁵ My frame was not hidden from you, when I was made in secret, *and* skillfully wrought in the lowest parts of the earth. ¹⁶ Your eyes saw my substance, being yet unformed. And in Your book they all were written, the days fashioned for me, when *as yet there were* none of them. (Psalm 139: 13-16)

We are triune beings made in his God's image. We have arrived at a human existence through some incredible odds.[xlviii]

According to doctors and scientists there is a greater chance of any of these happening than you being conceived in the womb:

- Man induced abortion during pregnancy prior to birth
- Winning the mega millions lottery
- Being Struck by lighting
- Being hit on the head by something falling out of the sky
- A ship capsizing in the middle of the ocean
- Accidently falling out of an airplane
- Death by choking on a chicken bone
- Being hit by a stray bullet

- Being trapped in the Caribbean and a hurricane bearing down on you

If you go back 10 generations (250 years) the chance of you being born at all is at most 1 divided by 6×10^{100} or

1 in 60000000000000000000000000000000 00000000000000000000000000 00000000000000000000000000000000.

In gambling, even a chance of 1 to 100 is not worth a gamble.   Each of us is tremendously blessed to have ever been born or be alive now! Even so we are in need of spiritual rebirth that only comes through placing our faith for eternity in Jesus Christ.

The Great Confession

Who is Jesus to you? Is he a good teacher? Is he a prophet? Is he one of the best people to ever live? Or is he who he declares himself to be? Do you see Jesus as the Lord of your life? To those of us who see Jesus as the Son Of God, and plant their faith in him, he gives the promise of everlasting life and resurrection at the last day. We will not be disappointed.

> "...but who do you say I am?" Simon Peter answered and said, **"You are the Christ, the Son of the living God."** Jesus answered and said to him, "Blessed are you, Simon Bar-jonah, for flesh and blood has not revealed this to you but my Father who is in heaven. Matthew 16:15-17

Life's most important question is what we will do with Jesus?

A confession is an absolute acknowledgement of truth. After one embraces a confession he/she lives with what follows, believing in their heart that all is well. Peter's vacillation

(Jesus rebukes him a short time later) after making the great confession reminds us that when we fall, God expects us to get back up. Consider John 6:66-70.

> From that *time* many of His disciples went back and walked with Him no more. [67] Then Jesus said to the twelve, "Do you also want to go away?" [68] But Simon Peter answered Him, "Lord, to whom shall we go? You have the words of eternal life. [69] Also we have come to believe and know that you are the Christ, the Son of the living God." [70] Jesus answered them, "Did I not choose you...?" John 6:66-70

There are times when life's pressures can make it seem easy to just deny (in word and/or deed) being affiliated with Jesus. The disciples that stopped hanging with Jesus did not go back into permanent sin, but they relapsed. Some Christians today are busy in work for Jesus Christ, but they do not walk with Him. The one thing God desires of us is an ongoing relationship with Jesus Christ. We must give God a clear and open path to our soul to do whatever he wants. We should not try to keep ourselves in relationship with Jesus by any other way, but living a natural life of absolute dependence on him as much as possible. Never try to live the life with God on any other term but God's terms, and those terms require absolute devotion to Him. The certainty that I do not know but God knows all—is a major handle of walking/going with Jesus.   Jesus wants to be our Savior and Lord, but he also wants us to be his partner in the kingdom harvest.

> Neither is there salvation in any other: for there is none other name under heaven given among men, whereby we must be saved. Acts 4:12

Where is salvation found? It is not found in our regrets or good works, because we could never be good enough to please a perfect God. It is not found in sincerity alone, because many religions and philosophies are sincere and yet diametrically opposed to each other and God's word. Where can salvation be found?

According to God's Word, it is found only in the perfect person and work of Jesus Christ. By his perfect life, selfless and substitutionary death, and powerful resurrection Jesus proved himself to be what he claimed to be during his life -- the one, true God. Salvation is found in him alone because he alone is able and willing to save us from our sins. I confess Jesus as my Savior and Lord.

> [32] "Therefore whoever confesses me before men, him I will also confess before My Father who is in heaven. [33] But whoever denies me before men, him I will also deny before My Father who is in heaven. Matthew 10:32-33

The Great Commandment

> ... "'You shall **love the Lord your God with all your heart, with all your soul, and with all your mind.**' [38] This is the first and great commandment. [39] And the second is like it: 'You shall **love your neighbor as yourself.**' [40] On these two commandments hang all the Law and the Prophets." Matthew 22:37-40

A commandment is non-negotiable. Following this supposition "The Great Commandment" is a part of God's hand on the disciple's life. These commandments are not only non-negotiable they are from God himself. They are not to be diluted or tweaked. These two commandments stand as is. Isn't God awesome? He ministers to us along life's journey and then allows us to minister to him in authentic worship.

Some may be old enough to remember various times in American life when different motifs for "who is my neighbor?" were more dominant than others. At one time who is my neighbor meant those who lived on the same farm. Then it meant those who lived on the same road. Later neighbors were those who lived on the same street. As multi-family housing began to proliferate, neighbor became defined as the person across the hall in the high-rise or in the same building. While each of these may have been/are cultural correct; they are all wrong from a biblical perspective no matter the point in time for usage. God would have us to know that any person of the human race is our neighbor and this is the biblical standard that we are to measure our actions by.

In the 22nd chapter of Matthew's Gospel, Jesus had dealt with one school of thinking (the Sadducees), sending them away to ponder what he had said. He now is confronted by a lawyer representing the Pharisees. Jesus disarms this legalist and all other legalists regarding the notion that we can be saved by the law. Jesus, our Savior, was needed then and he is needed now as the way, the truth and the light.

The mission field needs to know for what we stand. In general, western Christianity has done too good of a job letting the world know what we oppose. We don't have to compromise the Gospel to stand with God in love. When we stand for God in love we stand in God as we love people. There is a great truth in the song of the last century, "what the world needs now is love, sweet love." For God so loved the world that he gave his only son, that whosoever believes in him shall not perish but have everlasting life. God loves us enough that he didn't spare his son. He expects Christ followers (disciples) to love him with all of who we are. We are also to love other Christ followers (disciples) and those who have yet to understand the mission trip Jesus took from Heaven to earth. We show this love through intercessory prayer, living a life of obedience to God's word, and ministry.

The Great Commission

> "**Go therefore and make disciples** of all the nations, baptizing them in the name of the Father and of the Son and of the Holy Spirit, teaching them to observe all things that I have commanded you; and lo, I am with you always, even to the end of the age"   Matthew 28:19-20.

A commission is when one or a group is appointed to a task or a function by the prevailing authority. God has commissioned the Christ follower and the church to make disciples. A series of "All's" are used to give us the Great Commission.

1) "**All power**" - not limited to political, social, physical or economic power but Jesus declares that he has all power. Power to change circumstances and hearts.

2) "**All nations**" – Every person and all peoples are to be evangelized. God doesn't allow for selective evangelism.

3) "**All things**" commanded – God does not allow for limited scripture usage and teaching. Jesus commissions his disciples to observe "all things" he has commanded.

4) God is **"always"** with his disciples. This is a promise of presence directly from God. Not from man but from God. A promise of "I am" that means we don't have to wait to redeem or for redemption. He does not place this Godly promise somewhere in the future he makes it good right now. A promise of never ending extent. A promise of all circumstances. A promise of timelessness. A promise not just of yesterday or tomorrow but of the present day. There is no place or circumstance that can keep God away from us. When family and friends are gone, he's there. When enemies seem to prevail or leave he's still there. God's commissioned expectation has not and will not change.

Making disciples is more than just sowing the Gospel. Making disciples is so much more than being a religious funding mechanism. Making disciples is not about creating strong members of one political party or another. Making disciples, who are being taught "all things that Jesus commanded," means that every new disciple embraces being conformed to Christ likeness. Each disciple embraces a customized journey to eternity.

There are many good things that Christ followers and the church have evolved into doing in the 21st century; unfortunately, in some cases we have made these activities the main thing. There should be only one purpose for the Christ follower individually and in community. The one commissioned purpose is to make disciples. All else that we dare to do should be a means to this end.

Let's confess and repent over how we have allowed making disciples to get reduced to a part of the Kingdom enterprise instead of being the Kingdom enterprise. When disciple making is reduced to a segment it loses its rightful place as the umbrella for the other components. When disciple making is made a program it is minimized to classes, lectures and booklets. A disciple making lifestyle opens conversations for growth at all levels of Christian maturity.

Disciples are empowered by God through the Holy Spirit to teach. This does not mean that every born again believer should be able to step into the middle of a seminary level theological dialogue. It does mean that every believer is endowed with a testimony (a story) that no one else has. My story, like yours and all other Christ followers contains unique moments of understanding truth that God has chosen to unveil through my following him. As some have heard in the praise ditty…. "You can't tell it… let me tell it…

what the Lord has done for me." Every disciple should tell their testimony at every opportunity; God uses our sharing to multiply his message of love in America.

We celebrate what we measure. Baptism comes after the discipleship commitment, anything before this commitment is water play. The act of baptism does not bring about salvation. Every baptism is a public witness of life transformation. Christian converts, where possible, should always be given the opportunity to have the family of God celebrate with them as they symbolize arising in the newness of life. Baptisms should be counted and celebrated but not to the exclusion disciple making.

The Great Commission also embodies a tremendous promise. The promise is that our Lord will be with us always in every way and every place for the duration of the commission. So look back, he is in your past. Consider right now, he is with you in the present. With hope directly from God, look forward, he is already in your future, waiting on you.

A "Great Amen" closes the Great Commission. A closing of so it shall be done, affirmation, and agreement. The writer of this scripture would admonish us not to forget the Amen when God speaks. The great Commission closes with a GREAT AMEN.

The Great Charge (Assignment)

> "You shall receive power when the Holy Spirit has come upon you; and **you shall be witnesses to Me in Jerusalem, and in all Judea and Samaria, and to the end of the earth**" Acts 1:8

A charge is to assign a duty or responsibility to a person or to several people individually. Intermediate success should not interfere with our primary assignment. We often are able to see God do miraculous things as we are carrying out our assignment. Acts 1:8 is an assignment to the disciple and a synergistic collaboration to the body of Christ. Being a witness does not mean we are to convince people of God's reality. God does that himself. We are to be witnesses telling what the Lord has done in and for us (testimonies). Our greatest witnessing is the power of a transformed life.

The Acts 1:8 charge us geographic in regard to the world, from our backyards to the other side of the globe. In the American mission field we also have Acts 1:8 in urban fusion as peoples have immigrated from without and migrated within; global mission challenges are also within our nation's borders.

Acts 1:8 points out that the Holy Spirit has an empowering ministry. He directs us to where God would have us to be witnesses. He directs us to who God would have us to share a witness. He will also quicken us as to how we should share out of past experience, past equipping, and/or fresh encounters. As we pray and are sensitive to God's day to day; season to season; and life's journey directions we fulfill our assigned role in disciple making.

As in other parts of the New Testament, the Great Assignment is both historical and prophetic. It was for the Apostles and other early Christ followers as much as it is for you and me as disciples today. The Great Charge is also a witness of action and words.

The Great Charge is a specific and personal assignment to the believer. It is not to be delegated or vicariously carried out through resourcing another person alone. We also need not miss that the Great Charge is to be carried out in collaboration with other disciples. While we may never set foot in the ends of the earth, we can touch those areas through prayer and resource sharing. Modern technology provides a means for us to be even more engaged when one considers resources like improvements in air transportation quickness and safety as well as Google earth and voice as connecting and prayer resources.

We should support others in the Kingdom enterprise but not to the exclusion of the Lord's direct assignment to each of us. Acts 1:8 is corporate in as much as when individual disciples are obedient in fulfilling it the local church as well as the larger body of Christ is more and more robust.

At the end of the day all of God's Word is non-negotiable. It was written by men inspired of God and is God's revelation of himself to man. It is perfect in instruction. The word originates in God, salvation is its end, and it is truth, without any failure. God's word reveals the precepts by which God judges us, and therefore is, and will always be to the end of the world, the true center of Christianity, and the ultimate metric by which all human conduct should be tested. The great confession, the great commandment, the great commission, and the great charge are foundational truths from God's Word and not optional for the disciple.

The Great Consummation

> [15] For this we say unto you by the word of the Lord, that we which are alive and remain unto the coming of the Lord shall not prevent them which are asleep.[16] **For the Lord himself shall descend from heaven with a shout, with the voice of the archangel, and with the trump of God**: and the dead in Christ shall rise first:[17] Then we which are alive and remain shall be caught up together with them in the clouds, to meet the Lord in the air: and so shall we ever be with the Lord.   1 Thessalonians 4:15-17

There are two lens through which we need to see the Great consummation. The first is related to everyone that has, does, or will live in humanity. We all have a beginning, yes but we each have an ending. For those who have lived and are called to eternity before the return of the Lord Jesus, it is their personal great consummation. This understanding for the believer should be among the first prompts to the urgency of kingdom work even racial reconciliation – work while it is day because night is coming.

> ⁵ For the living know that they shall die: but the dead know not anything, neither have they any more a reward; for the memory of them is forgotten. ⁶ Also their love, and their hatred, and their envy, is now perished; neither have they any more a portion forever in any*thing* that is done under the sun. ⁷ Go thy way, eat thy bread with joy, and drink thy wine with a merry heart; for God now accepteth thy works. ⁸ Let thy garments be always white; and let thy head lack no ointment. ⁹ Live joyfully with the wife whom thou lovest all the days of the life of thy vanity, which he hath given thee under the sun, all the days of thy vanity: for that *is* thy portion in *this* life, and in thy labour which thou takest under the sun. ¹⁰ Whatsoever thy hand findeth to do, do *it* with thy might; for *there is* no work, nor device, nor knowledge, nor wisdom, in the grave, whither thou goest. Ecclesiastes 9:5-10

The second lens for viewing the Great Consummation is the return of the Lord Jesus on the last day. Paul shares with clarity about the last day. First the Lord himself in bodily form returns just as he left. So that no believer will miss his return event, the dead in Christ will get the first seats, followed by the believers that are still living. We will all meet the Lord in the air. This is awesome. But the greatest promise is that we will be with the Lord forever. No more separation. No more waiting. We will be done with the struggles of this world. This will be the great consummation of God's mission.

If we embrace the fact of one Heaven, doesn't it make sense to practice on this side of Glory what we will do in eternity? One day there will be **"The Great Consummation"** In the words of an American slave song – Jesus ain't comin' here t' die no mo.

Christians should embrace and live out our discipleship journey from a biblical worldview not a cultural Christianity worldview.[xlix] This action point is more difficult to measure as a metric regarding the impact on racial reconciliation as it is the umbrella for why we call ourselves Christians. It does point out the obvious in that if we deny any of the biblical worldview handles our entire framework collapses. For instance I can forget About the Acts 1:8 assignment if I do not embrace the Great Commandment. God is all about love. The Gospel is all about love. Having a biblical worldview is all about love. Racial reconciliation is all about love.

Chapter 6

Framing a Local Racial Reconciliation Process

Whether starting as an individual, local church, or some other faith community group; I have learned and observed that there are some common elements that frame any racial reconciliation process. The foundation of the ministry of reconciliation is our relationship with God and with other believers in the family of God. That's vertical and horizontal relationships. So in framing a reconciliation process the foundation is the cross. We get to the reconciliation portion of the cross through talking to God and each other.

Prayer – How God gives us the missional specifics

People who only pray sometimes will not arrive at the place of prayer that James 5:16 describes as "powerful and effective." It is powerful and effective prayer that America needs today in the 21st century. Let's be intentional about consistent praying together across all types of lines. This powerful prayer station also means we know how to do what Luke 6:27-28 tells us:

> But I say unto you which hear, Love your enemies, do good to them which hate you, bless them that curse you, and pray for them which despitefully use you.

It was interesting to discover the impact of praying this scripture and the application of this scripture by Dr. Martin Luther King Jr. as shared throughout the book entitled <u>Never to Leave Us Alone: The Prayer Life of Martin Luther King, Jr.</u>, by Lewis V. Baldwin.

We need to pray for strength to be obedient in all things. This means that pray is not to be used as a delay for those things it is already clear we should do. While in other matters still, we must obey in faith. So we pray to know what to do, the power to do it, and the faith to obey what we know to do.

It is through prayer and God's Word in the power of the Holy Spirit that we receive Godly revelation. We must accept that Godly revelation is not a democratic process nor should it be directed by the work of a pre-fabricated committee. Let's start praying. We learn to pray by praying. The more we pray, the better our prayers will be.

> …we must pray to pray, and continue in prayer so our prayers may continue…
> – Charles H. Spurgeon

We can stipulate that there is no missional activity without prayer. Prayer is even more important if we are to plant the Gospel together. Through prayer we are able to get on God's page of action and collectively move forward under the direction of one drum major. Satan knows the power of prayer so it is a major defense theater for him. He desires not only to kept us from individual prayer but especially block us from praying together as partners in the harvest.

Through prayer I have seen God save souls, give clear ministry direction, stay the hand of evil, open doors to ministry. We have been good, especially Christian leaders, in pleading for church members to be people of prayer, and our churches to be houses of prayer. This is ironic in that we as disciples who love Jesus should already be emphatic about hearing God.

As I understand prayer it should be more about us hearing God than our requesting of God. Herein is the deep question. Are we presenting God with a spiritual grocery list to keep a church or denomination in business or are we really seeking to hear his voice and standing ready to be obey "Him" until the mission is finished? Are we ready to give it all we have until our part on the continuum of the mission is finished?

Without Prayer ... Nothing happens. Little prayer=little revelation. Some prayer=some revelation. A precarious predicament though. Much prayer=much revelation. To see what God wants you to see it must be a matter of saturated individual and collective prayer. While serving as a Pastor in Memphis, Tennessee I had a placard outside of my office that said "If God deems prayer so essential why is it that we do so little of it? The most important part of the racial reconciliation process is to carry out a prayer actions. Prayer is not part of the strategy it is the strategy. It is not part of the battle it is the battle. We are mistaken if we think we should pray in the beginning and not pray throughout any season or focus. To state what maybe the obvious, prayer is our regular conversation with God and where we should do the most listening. Encourage those in your circles of influence to have an intentional active prayer life. When we allow our active prayer lives to cross pollinate, we see some awesome things happen for the kingdom's sake.

Ongoing Table Top Conversations

One of the side effects of segregation of all types is that we lose the art of conversation. The lowest common denominator of racial reconciliation is one on one conversation. I would encourage every believer to work on being a conversation starter in the power of the Holy Spirit. After all, Christ followers have something to share – the Gospel. As conversation starters we will have more possibilities for deeper conversations. These deeper conversations (table top conversations) are where relationships are built. Many ministry and mission ideas have come out of these conversations. It is through table top conversations that we can expand to larger groups for round table conversations. It is not acceptable to excuse not having cross racial conversations because we don't even have conversations within our particular race. We must have and encourage those in our circles of influence to be intentional about having table top conversations, trusting and allowing the Holy Spirit to do what he does. Praying, breaking bread, and talking moves us from knowledge of a person to understanding the person. From a process perspective table top conversations are not just to jump start the reconciliation process but are necessary to sustain an ongoing loving, interdependent environment.

Round Table Gatherings

As we engage vital one on one relationships across ethnicities and race, we are then in a position to expand our interactions to a larger group. Round table fellowships and huddles might include from a half dozen to a couple dozen people who connect with the purposes of prayer, fellowship, and missional action. The challenge with the expansion to do round table gatherings is to maintain the intentional purposes and prioritize the need for the gatherings. Many of us are too busy. Too busy with recreation activities in some cases. Too busy with doing good stuff that keeps us from doing great stuff in other cases. In still other times there are people who are busy doing nothing. As with one on one table top conversations; round table gatherings are not just doing for a time, but should be maintained as part of the reconciliation framework.

Reconciliation Worship and/or Revivals

After prayerfully considering the time that there has been a focus on table top conversations and round table gatherings; some approach to joint worship can be planned. These worship gatherings can take the form of an ongoing predetermined worship sharing cross pollinating different congregations or a multi-night revival type gathering that can also incorporate combined music and proclamation. Testimonies from cross racial prayer walking, witnessing and ministry should be a part of the services. The service also is a good time to highlight the area's table top conversation focus and roundtable gatherings. While these worships times are buoyed by table top conversations and round table gatherings; combined worship also can provide streams of possibilities back into opportunities for vital relationship building.

Reconciliation Conferencing and summits

With one on one interactions, small group interactions, combined worship times in play; it is good to consider sharing the big picture of what God is doing across a broader area. One format for such an annual public celebration, equipping, fellowship, and worship expression is a summit or conference highlighting the Gospel and racial reconciliation. While this type of event can be a lot of work; the energy and synergy generated in holding a conference or summit is significant.

Reconciliation/Collaboration Network(s) that continually carry out the previous steps.

During the 20th century, Christian denominations were able to thrive in the same separate but equal way of operating as the world. As with anything that is not of God, this too has passed. Denominations of all types and stripes are in decline. Another exposed aspect of denominational life are the claims to racial and ethnic diversity based on the number of churches. True diversity within denominational families is better measured by diverse congregations, diverse missionary forces, diverse elected officers, and diverse appointed officials (especially at the senior level). Diversity cannot be celebrated when an organization of several hundred has dozens of lower level workers mostly security and custodians and only one if any non-white senior level officials. The 21st century should see no only an increase in non-white elected (ceremonial positions) but more importantly an increase in the number of appointed positions that affect decisions, strategies, other personnel, and budgets. Until such changes happen we will continue to say we have a long way to go. To the extent that denominational families can make such changes, they will evolve and have relevance in the 21st century. To the extent denominational families don't address 21st century diversity realities, Gospel collaboration networks of various types are already developing and expanding to carry out the kingdom work in relevant ways.

> The eyes of the future are looking back at us and they are praying for us to see beyond our own time.[l]

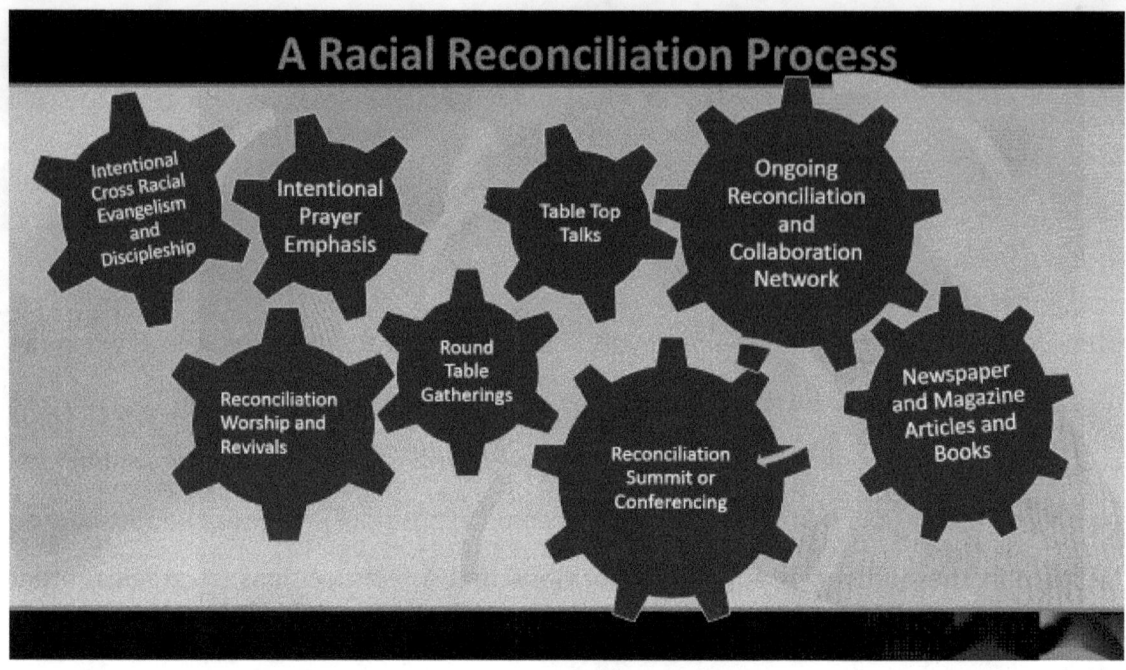

Americans are increasingly multi-generational, multi-racial, multi-ethnic, and multi-cultural and display many unique 21st century worldviews. A key factor in developing and maintaining a long-term relationship with those different from you is old-fashioned friendship built on trust, mutual respect and a desire for understanding. Don't allow differences (preferences) to become the basis for criticism and judgments. Racial differences are neither good nor bad. What we do with them is the key.

Missional strategy input that promotes reconciliation

- Determine actions that need to be stopped that hinder kingdom advancement.

- Develop and widely promote a shared current reality and Godly vision.

- Be intentionally inclusive (ethnically and innovatively). At all levels, we must share Prayer, Praise, Program, Pulpit, and Power.

- Invest in inclusive missional infrastructure at all levels of the denomination.

- Celebrate what God has done; historically, from the not distant past, and currently.

- Find ways to learn from other Christian family groupings, such as the Church of God In Christ, the United Methodist Church, and non-denominational churches.

- Lift up processes, patterns, principles, and practices from black ministry models

- Promote "indigenous leadership" development not "mission object ministry philosophy."

- Embrace a Kingdom view that includes a "Gospel collaboration" model.

- Create awareness of African Diaspora presence in Canada, Puerto Rico, and US Virgin Islands, and thus need to plant the Gospel among these "peoples."

Planting the Gospel in 21st Century America

- Planting the Gospel requires prayer.

- Planting the Gospel requires the right worldview i.e. a biblical one.

- Planting the Gospel cannot be done in local church or denominational isolation.

- Planting the Gospel requires truthful information and relevant information.

- Planting the Gospel requires the right missiological approaches

- Plant the Gospel to make disciples that leads to church growth & church multiplication.

- We can plant churches without planting the Gospel and thus have no kingdom or church growth.

- Gain an understanding of an allegory of church growth in Luke 5 for a team that leads to multiplication.

- Gain an understanding of an allegory of church growth in Acts 19 by a missionary landing in the city (Ephesus) planting the Gospel in spite of church leaders for area transformation.

- Planting the Gospel requires commitments to regular personal witnessing

12 actions within the body of Christ individuals can take to facilitate racial reconciliation.

- Embrace and live out our discipleship journey from a biblical worldview
- Pray toward an ever increasing prayer life.
- Have regular conversations in love and honesty. Not enough to just talk after a major challenge arises or an annual calendar day.
- Practice what we preach. Intentionally seek out and work on three individual relationships that you currently don't have or that are damaged: 1) In your family 2) In your church 3) Across racial lines
- Know more of the whole of Christian history.
- Teach and write more about the whole of Christian history especially in Bible colleges and seminaries.
- Learn missional principles across racial lines thus also helping cross denominational and nondenominational barriers.
- Work together toward kingdom impact with intentionality and specificity.
- When we resolve that everyone is welcome in our faith communities, get on with the business of sharing prayer, praise, program, proclamation and power.
- Determine what needs to be stopped and stop those things as much as lies within us.
- Hold each other accountable for what we should do.

APPENDIX

- **The Black National Anthem**

- **Black/ African-American History Month Facts for Features**

- **America's Black Population by state**

- **Puerto Rico's Black Population**

- **United States Virgin Islands Black Population**

- **Canada's Black Population by province**

- **Selected Internet Resources**

Lift Every Voice and Sing[li]

Lift ev'ry voice and sing,
'Til earth and heaven ring,
Ring with the harmonies of Liberty;
Let our rejoicing rise
High as the list'ning skies,
Let it resound loud as the rolling sea.
Sing a song full of the faith that the dark past has taught us,
Sing a song full of the hope that the present has brought us;
Facing the rising sun of our new day begun,
Let us march on 'til victory is won.

Stony the road we trod,
Bitter the chastening rod,
Felt in the days when hope unborn had died;
Yet with a steady beat,
Have not our weary feet
Come to the place for which our fathers sighed?
We have come over a way that with tears has been watered,
We have come, treading our path through the blood of the slaughtered,
Out from the gloomy past,
'Til now we stand at last
Where the white gleam of our bright star is cast.

God of our weary years,
God of our silent tears,
Thou who has brought us thus far on the way;
Thou who has by Thy might
Led us into the light,
Keep us forever in the path, we pray.
Lest our feet stray from the places, our God, where we met Thee,
Lest, our hearts drunk with the wine of the world, we forget Thee;

Shadowed beneath Thy hand,
May we forever stand,
True to our God,
True to our native land.

Lift Every Voice and Sing **- often called "The Black National Anthem"** - was written as a poem by James Weldon Johnson (1871-1938) and then set to music by his brother John Rosamond Johnson (1873-1954) in 1899. It was first performed in public in the Johnsons' hometown of Jacksonville, Florida as part of a celebration of Lincoln's Birthday on February 12, 1900 by a choir of 500 schoolchildren at the segregated Stanton School, where James Weldon Johnson was principal.

Black (African-American) History Month: February 2015[lii]

To commemorate and celebrate the contributions to our nation made by people of African descent, American historian Carter G. Woodson established Black History Week. The first celebration occurred on Feb. 12, 1926. For many years, the second week of February was set aside for this celebration to coincide with the birthdays of abolitionist/editor Frederick Douglass and Abraham Lincoln. In 1976, as part of the nation's bicentennial, the week was expanded into Black History Month. Each year, U.S. presidents proclaim February as National African American History Month.

Note: The reference to the black population in this publication is to single-race blacks ("black alone") except in the first section on "Population." In that section the reference is to black alone or in combination with other races; a reference to respondents who said they were one race (black) or more than one race (black plus other races).

Population
45.0 million -The number of blacks, either alone or in combination with one or more other races, on July 1, 2013, up 1.0 percent from July 1, 2012. Source: Population Estimates
http://factfinder2.census.gov/bkmk/table/1.0/en/PEP/2013/PEPSR5H?slice=Year~est72013
74.5 million -The projected black, either alone or in combination, population of the United States (including those of more than one race) for July 1, 2060. On that date, according to the projection, blacks would constitute 17.9 percent of the nation's total population. Source: Population projections Table 10
http://www.census.gov/population/projections/data/national/2014/summarytables.html
3.7 million -The black population in New York, which led all states as of July 1, 2013. Texas had the largest numeric increase since 2012 (78,000). The District of Columbia had the highest percentage of blacks (51.0 percent), followed by Mississippi (38.1 percent). Source: Population Estimates <http://www.census.gov/newsroom/press-releases/2014/cb14-118.html>
Follow @uscensusbureau on Twitter, Facebook, Flickr, YouTube and Ustream
1.3 million - Cook County, Ill. (Chicago) had the largest black population of any county in 2013 (1.3 million), and Harris, Texas (Houston) had the largest numeric increase since 2012 (18,000). Holmes, Miss., was the county with the highest percentage of blacks in

the nation (83.2 percent). Source: Population Estimates
http://www.census.gov/newsroom/press-releases/2014/cb14-118.html

Serving Our Nation
2.2 million-Number of black military veterans in the United States in 2013. Source: 2013 American Community Survey
http://factfinder.census.gov/bkmk/table/1.0/en/ACS/13_1YR/C21001B

Education
83.7% -The percentage of blacks 25 and over with a high school diploma or higher in 2013. Source: 2013 American Community Survey
http://factfinder.census.gov/bkmk/table/1.0/en/ACS/13_1YR/S0201//popgroup~004
19.3% -The percentage of blacks 25 and over who had a bachelor's degree or higher in 2013. Source: 2013 American Community Survey
http://factfinder.census.gov/bkmk/table/1.0/en/ACS/13_1YR/S0201//popgroup~004
1.7 million -Among blacks 25 and over, the number who had an advanced degree in 2013. Source: 2013 American Community Survey
http://factfinder2.census.gov/bkmk/table/1.0/en/ACS/13_1YR/B15002B
3.0 million -Number of blacks enrolled in undergraduate college in 2013 compared with 2.6 million in 2008, a 17.5 percent increase. Source: 2013 American Community Survey
http://factfinder2.census.gov/bkmk/table/1.0/en/ACS/13_1YR/B14007B
http://factfinder2.census.gov/bkmk/table/1.0/en/ACS/08_1YR/B14007B

Voting
17.8 million -The number of blacks who voted in the 2012 presidential election. In comparison to the 2008 election, about 1.7 million additional black voters reported going to the polls in 2012. Source: The Diversifying Electorate — Voting Rates by Race and Hispanic Origin 2012 http://www.census.gov/prod/2013pubs/p20-568.pdf
66.2% -Percent of blacks who voted in the 2012 presidential election, higher than the 64.1 percent of non-Hispanic whites who did so. This marks the first time that blacks have voted at a higher rate than whites since the Census Bureau started publishing statistics on voting by the eligible citizen population in 1996. Source: The Diversifying Electorate — Voting Rates by Race and Hispanic Origin 2012
http://www.census.gov/prod/2013pubs/p20-568.pdf

Income, Poverty and Health Insurance

$34,598 -The annual median income of black households in 2013, compared with the nation at $51,939. Source: U.S. Census Bureau, Income, Poverty and Health Insurance Coverage in the United States: 2013
http://www.census.gov/content/dam/Census/library/publications/2014/demo/p60-249.pdf

27.2% -Poverty rate in 2013 for blacks, while nationally it was 14.5 percent. Source: U.S. Census Bureau, Income, Poverty and Health Insurance Coverage in the United States: 2013
http://www.census.gov/content/dam/Census/library/publications/2014/demo/p60-249.pdf

84.1% -Percentage of blacks that were covered by health insurance during all or part of 2013. Nationally, 86.6 percent of all races were covered by health insurance. Source: U.S. Census Bureau, Health Insurance Coverage in the United States: 2013
http://www.census.gov/content/dam/Census/library/publications/2014/demo/p60-250.pdf

Families and Children

61.8% - Among households with a black householder, the percentage that contained a family in 2013. There were 9.8 million black family households. Source: 2013 Current Population Survey,

Families and Living Arrangements[liii]

45.7% - Among families with black householders, the percentage that were married couples in 2013. Source: 2013 Current Population Survey, Families and Living Arrangements, Table F1 http://www.census.gov/hhes/families/data/cps2013F.html 1.3 million - Number of black grandparents who lived with their own grandchildren younger than 18 in 2013. Of this number, 45.2 percent were also responsible for their care.[liv]

Jobs[lv]

28.1% - The percentage of civilian employed blacks 16 and over who worked in management, business, science and arts occupations, while 36.3 percent of the total civilian employed population worked in these occupations. Source: 2013 American Community Survey

How much do you know about the African Diaspora[lvi]

1. Africa is a: a) continent   b) country   c) peninsula
2. Which of the United States has the least number of Black Americans?
   a) Kansas   b) New York   c) Montana
3. Which of the United States has the highest percentage of Black Americans?
   a) Texas   b) Mississippi   c) Pennsylvania
4. Eric Holder, the first Black Attorney General of the United States, is of what ancestry?   a) Afro-Latino   b) African-Caribbean   c) Afro-European
5. What Caribbean country has the largest number of Black immigrants to the United States?   a) Haiti   b) Cuba   c) Jamaica
6. According to the most recent Canadian census, how many Black Canadians are there?
   a) less than 10,000   b) between 250,000-350,000   c) Just under 1 Million
7. Which NBA player is not African-American but Afro-European?
   a) Dwight Howard   b) Paul Pierce   c) Tony Parker
8. Who was the first man to die in the American Revolution? Hint: He was Black.
   a) George Washington Carver   b) Crispus Attucks   c) Ralph Ellison
9. Currently how many Blacks are serving as United States Senators?
   a) 25   b) 2   c) 7
10. Zipporah, was the Cushite Ethiopian wife of Moses. (Numbers 12). Who was her father?   a) Jayzee   b) John-Boy Walton   c) Jethro

UFN, Inc. (Answers provided in the Endnotes)

Black Population by State

	STATE	Black Population	%
1	New York	3,720,403	19%
2	Texas	3,489,003	13%
3	Florida	3,473,698	18%
4	Georgia	3,246,309	32%
5	California	2,930,846	8%
6	North Carolina	2,287,143	23%
7	Illinois	2,010,132	16%
8	Maryland	1,878,083	32%
9	Virginia	1,738,181	21%
10	Pennsylvania	1,614,965	13%
11	Ohio	1,596,723	14%
12	Louisiana	1,538,402	33%
13	Michigan	1,524,126	15%
14	New Jersey	1,410,324	16%
15	South Carolina	1,378,016	29%
16	Alabama	1,318,916	27%
17	Tennessee	1,164,579	18%
18	Mississippi	1,139,361	38%
19	Missouri	770,576	13%
20	Indiana	694,047	11%

21	Massachusetts	616,601	9%
22	Arkansas	483,411	16%
23	Connecticut	454,117	13%
24	Wisconsin	425,755	7%
25	Kentucky	402,129	9%
26	Washington	374,029	5%
27	Arizona	373,979	6%
28	Minnesota	368,583	7%
29	Oklahoma	353,195	9%
30	District of Columbia	329,875	51%
31	Nevada	289,946	10%
32	Colorado	285,072	5%
33	Delaware	220,106	24%
34	Kansas	217,769	8%
35	Iowa	128,813	4%
36	Oregon	112,916	3%
37	Nebraska	108,592	6%
38	Rhode Island	94,825	9%
39	West Virginia	82,322	4%
40	New Mexico	67,277	3%
41	Utah	54,856	2%
42	Hawaii	51,454	4%

43	Alaska	39,339	5%
44	New Hampshire	26,883	2%
45	Maine	24,737	2%
46	South Dakota	21,119	2%
47	Idaho	20,244	1%
48	North Dakota	17,127	2%
49	Wyoming	13,306	2%
50	Vermont	10,919	2%
51	Montana	10,536	1%

Source: 2013 US Census Bureau www.census.gov

Puerto Rico's Black Population[lvii]

Total Population Puerto Rico:	3,725,789
Total Black Population: (12%)	461,498
Black Male Population:	231,794
Black Female Population:	229,704
Black Population under 18 years:	124,115
Black Population 18 years and over:	296,332

Almost all Puerto Ricans have some African heritage. The actual racial statistics of Puerto Rico are not known, but research indicates that over 10% of Puerto Rico's population are pure blacks, with most of the island's population being mulatoes or mulato mixed with Native American lineage. Most pure blacks in Puerto Rico are found along the North Coast area (especially in the towns Loiza, Guayama, Ponce, and Carolina). Most Blacks are descended of African slaves brought from the Yoruba people of Nigeria.

The number of Puerto Ricans identifying themselves solely as black or American Indian jumped about 50 percent in the last decade, according to new census figures that have surprised experts and islanders alike. The increase suggests a sense of racial identity may be growing among the various ethnic groups that have long been viewed as a blurred racial mosaic on the U.S. territory, although experts say it is too soon to say what caused the shift. "It truly breaks with a historic pattern," said Jorge Duany, an anthropology professor at the University of Puerto Rico. The growth in those calling themselves black or American Indian reduced the population share of Puerto Ricans who identify themselves solely as white. That group dropped nearly 8 percentage points to about 76 percent of the island's 3.7 million people. More than 461,000 islanders identified themselves solely as black, a 52 percent increase, while nearly 20,000 said they were solely American Indian, an almost 49 percent increase. Experts said several factors could have influenced the rise in the number of people who identify themselves as black. Duany said the election of Barack Obama as U.S. president might have influenced some to call themselves black as the high-profile leader dispelled negative stereotypes about their race.[lviii]

US Virgin Island's Black Population[lix]

U.S. Virgin Islands, an unincorporated territory of the USA, claimed in 1917 (Islands of St. Thomas, St. Croix, and St. John. Capital City: Charlotte Amalie (18,914 pop.)   US Virgin Islands Population: 104,737 (*2013 estimated*)[lx]
black 79,810 (76.2%)
white 10,455 (13.1%)
Asian 878 (1.1%)
other 4,868 (6.1%)
mixed 2,793 (3.5%)

Languages: English 74.7%, Spanish or Spanish Creole 16.8%, French or French Creole 6.6%, other 1.9% (2000 census)

Religion: Protestant 59% (Baptist 42%, Episcopalian 17%), Roman Catholic 34%, other 7%

Age structure:

- 0-14 years: 18.2% (male 9,669/female 9,407)
- 15-24 years: 10.6% (male 5,075/female 6,063)
- 25-54 years: 39.3% (male 18,698/female 22,444)
- 55-64 years: 14.1% (male 7,036/female 7,750)
- 65 years and over: 17.8% (male 8,431/female 10,164) (2013 est.)

Median age: total: 43.5 years male: 43.7 years female:43.3 years (2013 est.)
Birth rate: 10.69 births/1,000 population (2013 est.)

Urbanization:
urban population: 95% of total population (2010)
rate of urbanization: -0.1% annual rate of change (2010-15 est.)

Black Canadians[lxi]

Province/Country	Blacks 2001	% 2001	Blacks 2011	% 2011	% change 2001-2011
Ontario	411,090	3.6%	539,205	4.3%	31% +
Quebec	152,195	2.1%	243,625	3.2%	60% +
Alberta	31,395	1.1%	74,435	2.1%	137% +
British Columbia	25,465	0.7%	33,260	0.8%	76% +
Nova Scotia	19,670	2.2%	20,790	2.3%	5.7% +
Manitoba	12,820	1.2%	19,610	1.7%	53% +
Saskatchewan	4,165	0.4%	7,255	0.7%	74% +
New Brunswick	3,850	0.5%	4,870	0.7%	26% +
Newfoundland and Labrador	840	0.2%	1,455	0.3%	73% +
Northwest Territories	175	0.5%	555	1.4%	217% +
Prince Edward Island	370	0.3%	390	0.3%	9.5% +
Nunavut	65	0.3%	120	0.4%	84.6% +
Yukon	120	0.4%	100	0.3%	17% -
Canada[lxii]	662,215	2.2%	945,665	2.9%	43% +

The next National Canadian Census will be conducted in 2016. National census are conducted every five years.

- About 30% of Black Canadians have Jamaican heritage.
- An additional 32% have heritage elsewhere in the Caribbean or Bermuda.
- 60% of Black Canadians are under the age of 35.
- 57% of Black Canadians live in the province of Ontario.
- 97% of Black Canadians live in urban areas.
- There are 32,000 more black women than black men in Canada.

Selected Internet Resources

American Religion Data Archives – www.thearda.com

Black Church and Denominations Information – www.theblackchurchpage.com

Brookings Institute - www.brookings.edu

Central Intelligence Agency Fact book online – www.cia.gov/cia/publications/factbook/

City Data – www.city-data.com

City/Community Information – www.usacitylink.com

Federal Bureau of Investigation (FBI) Uniform Crime Reports – www.fbi.gov

Federal Drug Enforcement Agency – www.dea.gov

Google Earth - www.google.com/earth/download

Migration Policy Institute – www.migrationpolicy.org

Pew Forum on Religion and Public Life – www.pewforum.org

Policom Corporation Maps and Economic Analysis - www.policom.com

Population Reference Bureau – www.prb.org

Rural Policy Institute - www.rupri.org

The Urban Institute - www.urban.org

US Census Bureau – www.census.gov

US Center for World Mission - www.joushuaproject.net

US Department of Homeland Security - www.dhs.gov/yearbook-immigration-statistics

US Department of Housing and Urban Development (HUD) – www.hud.gov

Bibliography

Alexander, Michelle, <u>The New Jim Crow, Mass Incarceration in the Age of Colorblindness</u>, The New Press, New York, 2010 and 2012.

Baldwin, Lewis V., <u>Never To Leave Us Alone, The Prayer Life of Martin Luther King Jr.</u>, Fortress Press, Minneapolis, Minnesota, 2010.

Black Aids Institute, <u>When we know better we do better</u>, Los Angeles, California, 2015.

Bonhoeffer, Dietrich, <u>The Cost of Discipleship</u>, Simon and Schuster, New York, New York, First Touchstone Edition 1995.

Bounds, E.M., <u>The Complete Works of E. M. Bounds on Prayer</u>, Baker Books, Grand Rapids, Michigan, 1990. Revised foreword 2004.

Children's Defense Fund Report, <u>America's Cradle to the Prison Pipeline</u>, Washington, D.C., 2007.

Ellison, Ralph, <u>Invisible Man</u>, Vintage Books, New York, New York, 1989 originally published 1952.

Evans, Tony, <u>America: Turning A Nation to God</u>, Moody Press, Chicago, Illinois, 2015.

Fitts, Leroy, <u>The Lott Carey Legacy of African American Missions</u>, Gateway Press, Baltimore, Maryland, Second Printing 1994.

Frey, William H., <u>Diversity Explosion, How New Racial Demographics are Remaking America</u>, Brookings Institution Press, Washington, D.C. 2015

Garrett, Chan C. compiler Home Mission Board, SBC, <u>Churches Ministering to Black America</u>, Atlanta, Georgia, 1987

Gates, Henry Louis Jr., <u>The African Americans, Many Rivers to Cross</u>, A PBS Film Documentary (DVD) 2013.

Gates, Henry Louis Jr., <u>Black in Latin America</u>, a PBS Film Documentary (DVD) 2011.

Gilbreath, Edward, Reconciliation Blues, A Black Evangelical's Inside View of White Christianity, Intervarsity Press, Downers Grove, Illinois, 2006.

Griffin, John Howard, Black Like Me, Signet Books, New York, New York, 1st printing 1962.

Hiebert, Paul G. The Gospel in Human Contexts, Anthropological Explorations for Contemporary Missions, Baker Publishing Group, Grand Rapids, Michigan, 2008.

Hiebert, Paul G. Transforming Worldviews, An Anthropological Understanding of How People Change, Baker Publishing Group, Grand Rapids, Michigan, 2008.

King, Martin Luther, Jr. Where Do We Go From Here: Chaos or Community? New York, NY: Harper & Row, 1967

Lincoln, C. Eric, Race, Religion and the Continuing American Dilemma, Revised Edition, Hill and Wang, New York, New York, 1999.

Lincoln, C. Eric and Mamiya Lawrence H., The Black Church in the African American Experience, Durham, North Carolina, Duke University Press, 2001.

Maston, T.B., The Bible and Race. Broadman Press Nashville, Tennessee, 1959.

McCall, Emmanuel, When All God's Children Get Together, A Memoir of Race and Baptist, Mercer University Press, Macon, Georgia, 2007.

McKissic Sr., William Dwight, Beyond Roots: In Search of Blacks in The Bible, Renaissance Productions, Inc., Wenonah, New Jersey, 1990.

McNairy, Chris, Missional Urban Fusion, Planting the Gospel in 21st Century America, Urban Fusion Network Books, Lawrenceville, Georgia, 2013.

McNairy, Chris, Christians Responding to America's Urban Fusion Realities, Urban Fusion Network Books, Lawrenceville, Georgia, 2013.

Morial, Marc H., 2014 State of Black America, One Nation Unemployed, Jobs Rebuild America, National Urban League, New York, New York, 2014.

National Advisory Commission on Civil Disorders, The Kerner Report, Bantam Books, New York, New York, 1968.

Salley, Columbus and Behm, Ronald, <u>What Color is Your God? Black Consciousness and the Christian Faith</u>, Carol Publishing Group, New York, New York, 1990.

Shannon, David T., <u>George Liele's Life and Legacy An Unsung Hero</u>, Mercer University Press, Macon, Georgia, 2012.

Simmons, Martha (Editor), Frank A. Thomas (Editor), <u>Preaching with Sacred Fire: An Anthology of African American Sermons, 1750 to the Present</u>, WW Norton and Company, New York, 2010.

Smiley, Tavis, Coordinator, <u>The Covenant</u>, Third World Press, Chicago, Illinois, 2006.

Smiley, Tavis, Coordinator, <u>The Covenant in Action</u>, companion to the book, The Covenant, The Smiley Group Incorporated, Carlsbad, California, 2006.

Taylor, Robert Joseph, Chatters, Linda M., Levin, Jeff, <u>Religion in the Lives of African Americans, Social, Psychological, and Health Perspectives</u>, Sage Publications, Thousand Oaks, California, 2004.

Thurston, Baratunde, <u>How to be Black</u>, Harper-Collins Publishers, New York, New York, 2012.

Warnock, Raphael G., <u>The Divided Mind of the Black Church, Theology, Piety and Public Witness</u>, New York University Press, New York, 2014.

Washington, Raleigh and Glen Kehrein, <u>Breaking Down Walls, A Model for Reconciliation in the Age of Racial Strife</u>, Moody Press, Chicago, Illinois, 1993.

West, Cornel, <u>Race Matters</u>, Vintage Books Edition, A Division of Random House Books, New York, New York, 2001.

Williams, Chancellor, <u>The Destruction of Black Civilization, Great Issues of Race from 4500 B.C. to 2000 A.D.</u>, Third World Press, Chicago, Illinois, 1987.

Williams, Terri M., <u>Black Pain, It Just Looks Like We're Not Hurting</u>, Scribner Books, New York, New York, 2008.

Wise, Tim, <u>White Like Me, Reflections on Race from a Privileged Son</u>, Berkley, California, 2008 and 2011.

Rev. Christopher "Chris" McNairy

Rev. Chris McNairy is the Facilitator of the Urban Fusion Network. The Urban Fusion Network (UFN) is a national network of likeminded Great Commission Christian peoples, churches, fellowships, other networks, and entities who synergistically focus on planting the Gospel, seek to enhance disciple making, and practice intentional urban missions collaboration. He has written <u>Missional Urban Fusion, Planting the Gospel in the 21st Century America</u> and the workbook, <u>Christians Responding to America's Urban Fusion Realities</u>. He has two forth coming resources <u>MAPPING – Missional Analysis of People, Places, Interests, Needs, and Godliness</u> and <u>A Jerusalem Pattern, Giving Proper Attention to Local Church Fields</u>.

Originally from Forrest City, Arkansas, Chris was saved as a teenager. An ordained Gospel minister (1985); he has served on local church staff, association, and state levels in Tennessee and Michigan.

Chris served in full time ministry with the North American Mission Board, SBC for over 12 years (2000-2012). He served the Baptist State Convention of Michigan as African American Ministries Leader 1998-2000. While serving in Tennessee (1988-1998); he served as Pastor of West haven Baptist Church in Memphis, Tennessee for 7 years (1992-1998); leading the church to start "Hope Centers in apartment communities" that still exist today as well as other innovative ministries. He speaks often in the areas of urban missions, Gospel planting and Diaspora research.

Previous Occasional Papers
"Mr. Chris Goes to Washington" – January 2013
"The SBC – How we are…How we need to be." June 2013
"Still afraid to have the race conversation?" December 2013
"Can we do the main thing?" February 2014
"Can you hear me now" June, 2014
"The Gospel – What is It? January 2015

urbanfusionnetwork@gmail.com

Endnotes

[i] Pastor James Dixon as reported in Baptist Press upon his election as President of the National African American President, SBC June 16, 2010.

[ii] Dr. John Upton Executive Director Baptist General Association of Virginia in *Kingdom Vision Revisiting the Race Question* webcast September, 2013.

[iii] Floyd calls Baptists to racially reconcile by Diana Chandler, posted Monday, December 15, 2014 http://www.bpnews.net/43917/floyd-calls-baptists-to-racially-reconcile

[iv] On December 7th, 1964, Dr. King gave a speech sponsored by the British group Christian Action about the civil rights struggle in the United States, as well as the anti-apartheid movement in South Africa. The speech was recorded by Saul Bernstein, who was working as the European correspondent for Pacifica Radio. Bernstein's recording was recently discovered by Brian DeShazor, director of the Pacifica Radio Archives.

[v] The Message (MSG) Copyright © 1993, 1994, 1995, 1996, 2000, 2001, 2002 by Eugene H. Peterson

[vi] Martin Luther King Jr Speech March 25, 1965 Montgomery Alabama; http://mlk-kpp01.stanford.edu/index.php/kingpapers/article/our_god_is_marching_on/ retrieved January 20, 2015.

[vii] From paper, The Gospel… what is it? By Rev. Chris McNairy January, 2015.

[viii] From Salem MB Church Notes from Sermon January 12, 1989.

[ix] The Inspirational Writings of C.S, Lewis in One Volume, Inspirational Press, New York, New York, 1994.

[x] http://news.yahoo.com/israel-biracial-german-author-probes-her-nazi-heritage-063034703.html Retrieved February 19, 2015.

[xi] http://www.juneteenth.com/history.htm Retrieved January 30, 2015.

[xii] From speech by Dr. Martin Luther King Jr. in St. Louis, Missouri, March 22, 1964.

[xiii] Still afraid to have the race conversation? An article by Chris McNairy December 18, 2013

[xiv] http://abacus.bates.edu/admin/offices/dos/mlk/letter.html Retrieved January 29, 2015.

[xv] Obama is not a Christian? By Timothy Stanley Updated 7:42 PM ET, Fri February 6, 2015 http://www.cnn.com/2015/02/06/opinion/stanley-prayer-breakfast-exceptionalism/index.html

[xvi] For whom the bell tolls a poem (No man is an island) by John Donne *poem - the passage is taken from the year 1624 Meditation 17, from Devotions Upon Emergent Occasions*

xvii http://www.biography.com/people/john-bunyan-9231294. John Bunyan." *Bio*. A&E Television Networks, 2014. Web. 19 Dec. 2014.
xviii http://www.pbs.org/wgbh/aia/part3/3p97.html# retrieved December 19, 2014
xix *Biographical Dictionary of Evangelicals.* Timothy Larsen, editor. Downers-Grove, Illinois: Intervarsity Press, 2003.
xx Shannon, David T., George Liele's Life and Legacy An Unsung Hero, Mercer University Press, Macon, Georgia, 2012.

xxi http://www.biography.com/people/jonathan-edwards-9284916 Jonathan Edwards." *Bio*. A&E Television Networks, 2014. Web. 19 Dec. 2014.
xxii Fitts, Leroy, The Lott Carey Legacy of African American Missions, Gateway Press, Baltimore, Maryland, Second Printing 1994.
xxiii http://www.sbhla.org/bio_anniearmstrong.htm retrieved December 18, 2014
xxiv Margaret Washington, Sojourner Truth's America (Illinois, 2009)
xxv Harper, Keith, ed. (2002). *Send the Light: Lottie Moon's Letters and Other Writings.* Macon, Ga.: Mercer University Press
xxvi http://www.dacb.org/stories/congo/fleming_louise.html retrieved December 18, 2014
xxvii http://biographybasics.blogspot.com/2008/11/robert-green-lee-baptist-preacher-born.html retrieved January 27, 2015
xxviii Nick Salvatore, *Singing in a Strange Land: C. L. Franklin, the Black Church, and the Transformation of America*, Little Brown, 2005
xxix http://www.nytimes.com/1995/12/02/us/herschel-h-hobbs-88-southern-baptist-leader.html retrieved December 18, 2014
xxx http://www.nytimes.com/1987/10/18/obituaries/rev-w-h-brewster-gospel-song-composer.html retrieved December 18, 2014
xxxi Michael J. Martin, *Dietrich Bonhoeffer*. Champion of Freedom series. (Morgan Reynolds Publishing, 2012).
xxxii Fleming, Alice, Martin *Luther King, Jr.: A Dream of Hope*. Sterling, (2008).
xxxiii http://www.lwf.org/site/PageServer?pagename=abt_AboutAdrianRogers retrieved January 27, 2015
xxxiv http://www.bcnn1.com/gardnerctaylor/ retrieved December 18, 2014
xxxv http://billygraham.org/ December 28, 2014
xxxvi http://www.preaching.com/resources/past-masters/11671785/ retrieved December 18, 2014
xxxvii http://gaither.com/ retrieved February 8, 2015

xxxviii http://www.usatoday.com/story/life/music/2015/01/08/andrae-crouch-gospel-music-pioneer-dies/21262183/ retrieved February 18, 2015

xxxix https://www.rodparsley.com/ retrieved February 18, 2015

xl http://www.trinityfi.org/press/tdjakes01.html retrieved December 28, 2014

xli http://www.davidjeremiah.org/site/ retrieved December 28, 2014

xlii http://www.franklinabc.com/ retrieved February 8, 2015

xliii http://www.joelosteen.com/Pages/Home.aspx retrieved February 8, 2015

xliv http://www.nytimes.com/2009/05/24/nyregion/24pastor.html?pagewanted=all&_r=0 retrieved December 28, 2014

xlv The Financial Consequences of Saying 'Black,' vs. 'African American' People make vastly different assumptions about salary, education, and social status depending on which phrase is used. Joe Pinsker Dec 30 2014,

http://www.theatlantic.com/business/archive/2014/12/the-financial-consequences-of-saying-black-vs-african-american/383999/

xlvi National Broadcasting Company (NBC) coverage of the 2013 French Open Women's Tennis Championship. Aired June 8, 2013.

xlvii Substantial portions of this chapter first appeared in Missional Urban Fusion, Planting the Gospel in 21st Century America, Rev. Chris McNairy, Urban Fusion Network Books, Lawrenceville, Georgia 2013.

xlviii http://www.huffingtonpost.com/dr-ali-binazir/probability-being-born_b_877853.html Posted: 06/16/2011 3:58 pm EDT Updated: 08/16/2011 5:12 am EDT

xlix Biblical Worldview graphic and pattern of associating scriptures from work of Urban Fusion Network, Inc. Latest revision December, 2014.

l From the introduction of book Smiley, Tavis, Coordinator, The Covenant, Third World Press, Chicago, Illinois, 2006.

li http://www.pbs.org/black-culture/explore/black-authors-spoken-word-poetry/lift-every-voice-and-sing/ Retrieved January 15, 2015

lii Editor's note: The presented data were collected from a variety of sources and may be subject to sampling variability and other sources of error. Facts for Features are customarily released about two months before an observance in order to accommodate magazine production timelines. Questions or comments should be directed to the Census Bureau's Public Information Office: telephone: 301-763-3030; e-mail: pio@census.gov .

[liii] Table HH-1 and F1 http://www.census.gov/hhes/families/data/cps2013H.html
[liv] Source: 2013 American Community Survey
http://factfinder2.census.gov/bkmk/table/1.0/en/ACS/13_1YR/B10051B
[lv] http://factfinder2.census.gov/bkmk/table/1.0/en/ACS/13_1YR/S0201//popgroup~004
http://factfinder2.census.gov/bkmk/table/1.0/en/ACS/13_1YR/S0201
[lvi] **Answers 1-a, 2-c, 3-b, 4-b, 5-c, 6-c, 7-c, 8-b, 9-b, 10-c**
[lvii] https://suburbanstats.org/population/how-many-people-live-in-puerto-rico
[lviii] Associated Press
http://www.nativetimes.com/index.php?option=com_content&id=5143:puerto-rico-sees-increase-in-blacks-american-indians&Itemid=27
[lix]
http://www.worldatlas.com/webimage/countrys/namerica/caribb/usvirginislands/vifacts.htm
[lx] 2013 World Fact Book, an information web based source of the American government Central Intelligence Agency   http://www.cia.gov/cia/publications/factbook/
[lxi] Statistics Canada Comparison of 2001 and 2011 Census www.st atcan.ca

[lxii] At times, it has been substantiated that Black Canadians have been significantly undercounted in census data. A McGill University study which found that fully 43 per cent of all Black Canadians were not counted as black in the 1991 Canadian census, because they had identified themselves on census forms as British, French or other cultural identities which were not included in the census group of Black cultures. Although subsequent censuses have reported the population of Black Canadians to be much more consistent with the McGill study's revised 1991 estimate than with the official 1991 census data, no recent study has been conducted to determine whether some Black Canadians are still substantially undercounted. According to the 2011 Canadian Household Survey the official Black Canadian Population in 2011 was 945,665. Canada's population was estimated at 35,675,800 on October 1, 2014,
up 135,400 (+0.4%) from July 1, 2014, according to preliminary population estimates, which are now available for the third quarter by province and territory.[lxii] While Canadian officials don't estimate groups within the general population **the Urban Fusion Network estimate of the current Black Canadian population is well over 1.3 Million.** This estimate is based on calculations of Statistics Canada's visible minority counts.

www.ingramcontent.com/pod-product-compliance
Lightning Source LLC
Chambersburg PA
CBHW050452110426
42744CB00013B/1970